Opening up
Romans

PETER CURRIE

DayOne

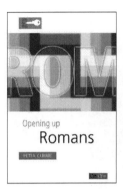

Opening up
Romans

PETER CURRIE

The Apostle Paul's epistle to the Romans has been one of the most crucial cornerstones that has shaped the history of the world. Perhaps in Romans more than any other book of Scripture do we discover the core mechanics of the gospel, our salvation in Christ Jesus and a deep knowledge of God.

To study Romans is therefore to know God and worship Him. I am very thankful for Peter's hard work in developing this short commentary that will be accessible to any believer at any stage of the Christian life. Peter very helpfully and simply walks the reader through the development of the Apostle Paul's mind as he expounds the gospel of Christ Jesus. Anyone that picks up this commentary will certainly discover the riches of Jesus and emerge knowing the Lord better.

Gavin Kinnaird, Co-Pastor at Trinity Road Chapel, London

Copyright © 2022 by DayOne Publications

First published in Great Britain in 2022

British Library Cataloguing in Publication Data
A record for this book is available from the British Library

ISBN: 978-1-84625-711-7

Printed by 4edge

DayOne, Ryelands Road, Leominster, HR6 8NZ
Email: sales@dayone.co.uk
Website: www.dayone.co.uk

Dedication
To Dr Martin Luther, with profound respect, who
grasped the great truth that 'the just shall live by faith'
and then rose up and shook Europe.

6

Contents

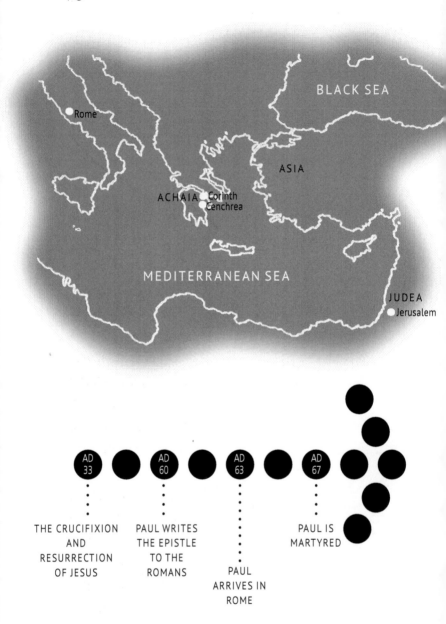

BLACK SEA

ASIA

ACHAIA Corinth
Cenchrea

MEDITERRANEAN SEA

JUDEA
Jerusalem

AD 33 — THE CRUCIFIXION AND RESURRECTION OF JESUS

AD 60 — PAUL WRITES THE EPISTLE TO THE ROMANS

AD 63 — PAUL ARRIVES IN ROME

AD 67 — PAUL IS MARTYRED

Overview

The apostle Paul's 'epistle', or letter to the Romans, is rightly placed first among the New Testament epistles. It was not the first to be written, but it is the fullest and most systematic explanation of the Christian gospel found anywhere in the Bible and it should be read and understood by every Christian. The great reformer, Martin Luther, said that it 'can never be read or pondered too much'[1] and the great translator and martyr, William Tyndale, said that it is the 'principal and most excellent part of the New Testament'[2].

Richard De Haan, the well-known Bible teacher, rightly said that 'a serious study of Paul's epistle to the Romans can be a life-transforming experience'[3]. I hope and pray that this will be the experience of my readers. Unless otherwise indicated, all quotations are from the New King James Version.

Finally, some advice. This commentary is not a substitute for the Bible! Make sure you read carefully the relevant verses in each section of Romans and also the cross-references I give to other parts of the Bible. Then read what I say, to help you understand Romans better, and 'may the God of hope fill you with all joy and peace in believing, that you may abound in hope by the power of the Holy Spirit' (Romans 15:13).

Background and summary

According to legend, the city of Rome was founded by Romulus in 753 BC. In those days, the great empire, in proximity to the land of Israel, was the Assyrian Empire. This was followed by the Babylonian Empire, which was in turn followed by the Persian Empire. These empires were all based in the Middle East. However, the next empire came from the West. In 331 BC, Alexander the Great's army of 47,000 men met the massive Persian army of Darius III near Gaugamela, close to the modern city of Dohuk in Iraqi Kurdistan. The Persian army numbered half a million, but Alexander drove them into headlong retreat.

Just eight years later, Alexander died of malarial fever, but Greek influence controlled the Middle Eastern lands for almost two centuries. However, further west, two other empires were rising: one based in the North African city of Carthage; the other based in Rome. Eventually, Rome prevailed over Carthage and conquered Greece as well. By the time our Lord Jesus Christ was born in Bethlehem of Judea, the Roman Empire controlled most of the lands surrounding the Mediterranean Sea and the remainder was annexed during the course of the next one hundred years or so.

The Roman Empire was pagan and polytheistic and

Christianity was fiercely persecuted from the time of Nero (AD 67, according to *Foxe's Book of Martyrs*[1]) onwards, until Constantine the Great introduced religious tolerance for Christianity in AD 313. However, the so-called 'Pax Romana'—the peace which existed between nationalities within the Roman Empire—did facilitate the great missionary journeys of the apostle Paul. Also, he himself was a Roman citizen, owing to him being born in Tarsus in Cilicia (see Acts 22:27–29), which gave him certain privileges.

Paul had a great desire to visit Rome and preach the gospel there. However, it is a good thing that his visit to Rome was delayed, because otherwise this great epistle to the Romans might never have been written! The epistle is thought to have been written when Paul was in Corinth in about AD 60, according to Archbishop Ussher, the great chronologist[2]. It may well be that a woman named Phoebe was the bearer. She was 'a servant of the church in Cenchrea', which is near Corinth, and she had business of some sort to transact in Rome (see Romans 16:1–2). Paul himself eventually arrived in Rome as a prisoner in about AD 63, according to Ussher.

Greeting to the Christians in Rome (1:1–7)

The epistle to the Romans is in three main parts. In his book, *Explore the Book*[3], Dr J. Sidlow Baxter helpfully sets it out thus:

- Doctrinal: How the gospel saves the sinner (chapters 1–8)
- National: How the gospel relates to Israel (chapters 9–11)
- Practical: How the gospel bears on conduct (chapters 12–16)

It can readily be seen from this division that the great theme of the whole epistle is *the gospel*. The words, 'the gospel', occur four times in the opening section of seventeen verses.

1 The Gospel

(1:1–17)

As we come to a verse-by-verse examination of Romans, we may well remind ourselves of the great truth that 'All Scripture is given by inspiration of God and is profitable' (1 Timothy 3:16a). God has spoken through His Word, and this epistle contains some of the most important teaching He has ever given to mankind. It will be well for us, therefore, to approach the study of it in a humble and prayerful spirit.

The apostle Paul starts by saying that he is 'a bondservant of Jesus Christ', sent forth by his Lord to proclaim, 'the gospel of God' (1:1). However, there is no reluctance or compulsion in true Christian service. The Bible is clear that 'God loves a cheerful giver' (2 Corinthians 9:7) and that 'faith [works] through love' (Galatians 5:6). Paul loved his Saviour and most willingly gave himself to this great task of proclaiming the gospel of God.

The Greek word translated as 'gospel' means 'good

message' or 'good news'. The opening verses tell us three things about this good message:

- It is God's good message (1:1)
- It is based on the Old Testament (1:2)
- It is about 'His Son Jesus Christ our Lord' (1:3a)

Humanly speaking, the Lord Jesus Christ is the promised King descended from David (1:3b), but He is also 'declared to be the Son of God with power' (1:4a)—the One who is equal with God the Father. Jesus Himself said that 'all should honour the Son just as they honour the Father' (5:23a; also see John 5:18). The Resurrection proves that our Lord's claims are true—He is 'declared to be the Son of God with power according to the Spirit of holiness, *by the resurrection from the dead'* (1:4).

The expression, 'according to the Spirit of holiness', reflects the fact that the Holy Spirit played a part in raising Jesus from the dead (see 8:11). Also, after our Lord was raised from the dead, He Himself said, 'All authority has been given to me in heaven and on earth' (Matthew 28:18), and part of that authority, part of that power, was the sending of the Holy Spirit on the Day of Pentecost to empower His disciples for world mission. This links up with what Paul says next:

> Through Him [Jesus the Son of God] we have received grace and apostleship for obedience to the faith among all nations (1:5a).

Paul was sent forth to proclaim the gospel, to the

end that some from every nation should be *obedient to the faith* by putting their trust in the Lord Jesus Christ as their Saviour. This is not only to meet our need, but also 'for His name' (1:5b)—to exalt the great name of our Lord Jesus Christ.

The gospel is calling out a company of people from all nations, including the Christians at Rome (1:6). They are 'called to be saints' (1:7a), just as Paul was 'called to be an apostle' (1:1). This applies to all who are genuinely trusting in the Lord Jesus Christ as their Saviour. Some of us are not as saintly as we should be, but we all belong to this set-apart company of people who will one day stand before the throne of God and the Lamb, and, with jubilant voices, will praise Him for their salvation (see Revelation 7:9–10).

> He has a mighty heart of love that 'desires all men to be saved'.

Another thing about all who are genuinely trusting in the Lord Jesus Christ as their Saviour is that we are 'beloved of God' (1:7a). God loves all mankind—He has a mighty heart of love that 'desires all men to be saved' (see 1 Timothy 2:3–4). However, those who *are saved* become born-again children of God and then we experience the fullness of His love (see 1 John 3:1a). How great is the love with which God loves those who are genuinely trusting in the Lord Jesus Christ as their Saviour!

Paul concludes the first paragraph of the introduction with a greeting—'Grace to you and peace from God our Father and the Lord Jesus Christ' (1:7b). Were he addressing non-Christians, this would probably refer to saving grace and peace with God. However, this is a greeting to the 'saints' who already have these blessings (see Ephesians 2:8 and Romans 5:1). Therefore, I think Paul has in mind *strengthening* grace and the peace *of God* (see 2 Corinthians 12:9a; Philippians 4:6–7). These blessings come to us equally 'from God our Father and the Lord Jesus Christ' (1:7b), and Geoffrey Wilson rightly comments that 'the juxtaposition of these names is further proof that the absolute Deity of Christ was of the very essence of Paul's gospel'.[1]

Paul thanks God for them and expresses his desire to see them (1:8–15)

Paul begins the second paragraph of chapter one by thanking God for their faith (1:8)—this is appropriate because we cannot come to the Lord Jesus Christ and put our trust in Him without God's help; by nature, sinners run away from God (see Genesis 3:8; John 3:20). However, as well as thanking God for the Christians, Paul prays for them (we all need praying for!), and says he wants to visit them. In fact, this was one of the things he prayed about (1:9–10). Sometimes, we can be the answer to our own prayers, and this is what Paul wanted.

He wanted to visit them and do them good spiritually (1:11), but he expected that they would do him good too (1:12)—every Christian can do something to encourage their fellow-believers.

So far, Paul had been unable to visit them, but he had been sent forth to proclaim the gospel to the Gentiles and he wanted to 'have some fruit among you, just as among the other Gentiles' (1:13; see also Acts 26:17–18). Paul's commission included all nations and all types of people (1:14), and so he was 'ready to preach the gospel to you who are in Rome also' (1:15).

The gospel in a nutshell (1:16–17)

The gospel is Paul's great theme. He says, 'I am not ashamed of the gospel of Christ' (1:16a), meaning that he is very proud of it. This is because he knows that it is 'the power of God to salvation for everyone who believes' (1:16a). Every word of this statement is significant. Note well the following emphases which show that the gospel of Christ is:

- powerful—it is 'the *power* of God to salvation for everyone who believes'
- divine—it is 'the power of *God* to salvation for everyone who believes'
- saving—it is 'the power of God to *salvation* for everyone who believes'

- unique—it is '*the* power of God to salvation for everyone who believes'
- universal—it is 'the power of God to salvation for *everyone* who believes'.

Faith is the channel by which the blessing comes to us—it is 'for everyone who *believes*'. We believe the message to be true and we put our trust in the Saviour of whom it speaks.

> Faith is the channel by which the blessing comes to us.

The gospel was 'for the Jew first' because the Jews were the Old Testament people of God. However, it is not 'for the Jew only', but 'also for the Greek' (1:16b). In fact, it is for all nations and all types of people—it is for everyone.

The Jewish priority was observed historically in the book of Acts, but the majority of the Jewish people rejected the wonderful message of salvation. Therefore, now, God has turned to the Gentiles (this was always His intention) and the great 'whosoever will' (Revelation 22:17 KJV) message is going to the uttermost part of the earth, saving many (see Acts 13:46–48). However, God still loves the Jewish people, as we shall see when we look at chapters 9–11.

The gospel is a message about the Lord Jesus Christ, as I have said already, and 'in [this message] ... the righteousness of God is revealed' (1:17a). This is not the righteousness of God in punishing sinners, but *in justifying them* (i.e., declaring them *righteous* or *not guilty*), as we shall see in chapter 2. It was when Martin Luther understood this, that Romans became the gate of heaven for him. This righteousness is 'from faith to faith' or 'by faith to faith'—the latter is the literal rendering, according to Robert Haldane.[2] I think this means that this way of justifying sinners *by faith* is revealed in the gospel and it is offered *to faith*, that is to whoever is willing to trust in Jesus Christ as their Saviour.

Anyway, it is clear that faith and trust in the Lord Jesus Christ is the only condition of salvation. The quotation from Habakkuk 2:4, 'The just shall live by faith', confirms this (1:17b). This is a great Old Testament proof text, showing that the gospel was indeed 'promised before ... in the Holy Scriptures' (1:2). It is quoted three times in the New Testament (see Galatians 3:11; Hebrews 10:38–39) and it is a fitting climax to the apostle's introductory remarks. *The just shall live by faith!* This includes a righteous standing before God plus new life in Christ. These blessings are ours simply by trusting in Him as our Saviour.

For further study ▶

FOR FURTHER STUDY

1. Paul wanted to visit the Roman Christians and do them good, but he expected that they would do him good too. Look at Galatians 6:1–10 to find examples of what he may have had in mind.

2. Paul gives us the gospel in a nutshell in 1:16–17. Look at other 'nutshell' statements such as John 3:16; 1 Corinthians 15:3–4; Ephesians 2:8–9; and 1 Timothy 1:15.

TO THINK ABOUT AND DISCUSS

1. What does the Bible teach about the ways in which we should love and do good to one another?

2. What is the value of short pithy summary statements concerning our faith?

2 The whole world guilty before God

(1:18–3:20)

As we continue in our study of this epistle, the reader may well be tempted to skip over this section in order to advance immediately to the wonderful, positive teaching beyond. However, we should bear in mind that we only really appreciate the good news of Christ in proportion, as we are thoroughly convinced of our need of it. This is Paul's purpose in the verses we are about to consider.

As we begin to read this section we are immediately confronted with a big change of emphasis—gospel sunshine is replaced by the storm clouds of 'the wrath of God' (1:18). This is because the apostle wants to prove the sinfulness of all mankind (3:9) and the impossibility of being saved by anything we do (3:20)—people do not feel their need for the gospel until they are convinced that they are sinners who are unable to save themselves.

The wrath of God is His righteous anger because of

'ungodliness and unrighteousness' (1:18). Ungodliness is the first and the worst—this refers to our sinful attitude towards God. However, God is also concerned about our sinful attitude towards people—His anger is against all that is wrong and the Bible says that a Day of Judgment is coming, 'the day of wrath and revelation of the righteous judgment of God', when every wrong will be put right (2:5; see also Acts 17:30–31).

The pagan world guilty before God (1:18–32)

On that day, the wrath of God will be fully revealed, but Paul says that it is revealed to some extent even now (1:18a). I believe this includes God's past judgments such as the Flood and the destruction of Sodom and Gomorrah, and also the fact that God has shown His anger by giving up the pagan world to a degraded lifestyle (see 1:24; 1:26; 1:28).

This is because the pagan world rejected the truth about God (1:18–20). We need only to look around at 'the things that are made' to realise that there must be a great God who made them. The argument from design is so strong that those who reject it are 'without excuse' (1:20). (The expression 'the things that are made' is just one word, *poiema*, in Greek. Our English word *poem* is derived from it. The same word appears in Ephesians 2:10, where it is translated 'workmanship'.)

To start with, the truth about God shone forth and the

next verse says, 'they knew God' (1:21a). However, this knowledge was unwelcome and a few verses later Paul says, 'they did not like to retain God in their knowledge' (1:28a). They did not want to give to God the glory due to His Name, nor to thank Him for His goodness towards them (1:21a; see also Acts 14:17). Therefore, their ideas about God became foolish, even though they claimed to be wise (1:21b–22).

Paul is talking about how the pagan world developed from early times until his day, but it is much the same today, only worse. In the West, especially, not only the truth about God, but also the Christian gospel has shone forth for centuries. However, 'the light of the knowledge of the glory of God in the face of Jesus Christ' (2 Corinthians 4:6) is unwelcome to many and so they are turning to darkness and foolishness.

Paul says that in early times people started to think that the great and holy God was like themselves, or even like animals (1:22–23; the plurality shows how polytheism began). Therefore, God gave them up to a degraded lifestyle (1:24)—because they rejected the truth about God and did not give God His rightful place in their lives (1:25). This degraded lifestyle included homosexuality. The apostle calls such behaviour 'vile', 'against nature' and 'shameful' (1:26–27). Moreover, he says that people who do such things suffer not only on the Day of Judgment, but even here and now (1:27b).

By focusing on homosexuality, Paul does not necessarily mean that it is the worst sin, and it is certainly not unforgivable (see 1 Corinthians 6:9–11). However, it *is* a violation of the natural order ('against nature') and as such it is a striking illustration of how mankind has turned away from what God ordained in the beginning (see Genesis 1–2).

As well as homosexuality, many other things are listed in 1:28–31, some of which are strikingly up to date. The terrible climax is when people who know better do these very wrong things and, worse still, are pleased when others do them too (1:32).

Pagan moralists also guilty before God (2:1–16)

Chapter 1 ends with the apostle referring to people not only doing wrong things themselves but also being pleased when others do them too. However, not everyone seems to fall into that category. I think some Gentile, non-Christians in Paul's day would have replied, 'I agree with you. Such people deserve to be punished. But I am different. I speak out against such practices.' However, Paul is not fooled by such people. They may appear to be respectable, decent and law-abiding, but they too are sinners (2:1). Paul is not fooled by such people and neither is God (2:2).

Such people will not 'escape the judgment of God' (2:3). Speaking out against sin is no substitute for repentance. This is what God wants us to do. This is why the Day of Judgment is delayed. It is to give us time to repent (2:4; see also 2 Peter 3:9).

When we think of this good and patient God waiting for us to repent, it should move us to run to Him and say sorry and mean it, but instead people are hard-hearted and the Day of Judgment draws ever nearer when God 'will render to each one according to his deeds' (see 2:5–6).

> When we think of this good and patient God waiting for us to repent, it should move us to run to Him and say sorry and mean it.

If we were to do good, then the reward would be eternal life, but this is a hypothetical case, because 'patient continuance' is required (2:7). We would have to do good every day of our lives without a single lapse (see Galatians 3:10). In chapter 3, Paul concludes that nobody like this exists. All are 'under sin' (3:9). 'There is none who does good, no, not one' (3:12).

In this case, what are we to expect? 'Indignation and wrath, tribulation and anguish', says Paul (2:8–9a). God hates sin—He is indignant and angry—and the execution of His justice will mean tribulation and anguish for sinners. Hell is 'the everlasting fire' where sinners will feel the heat of God's anger forever (Matthew 25:41). This will include being banished from His presence and experiencing everlasting anguish and torment (see Revelation 20:10).

This judgment applies to both Jews and Gentiles (2:9b–11), but it will be fair and according to what people know. The Jewish people who know about the law of God will be judged according to a higher standard than pagan Gentiles who only have the light of creation and conscience (2:12; see also Luke 12:47–48).

This will happen at the second coming—'in the day when God will judge the secrets of men by Jesus Christ, according to my gospel' (2:16). Not only will words and deeds be examined, but also 'the secrets of men'—the thoughts and motives of our hearts. 'Man looks at the outward appearance, but the Lord looks at the heart' (1 Samuel 16:7b). Before the Flood, it was when God saw what was in the hearts of the people of those days that He was so grieved (see Genesis 6:5–6).

The Jewish people were proud of the fact that they knew better than the Gentiles, but this did not justify them before God (2:13). They knew what was right, but they did not always do what was right, as we shall see. By contrast, the pagan Gentiles, even though they did not know about the Ten Commandments, showed by their behaviour that something was going on within them. This is because everyone has a conscience—that part of us which distinguishes between right and wrong (2:14–15). Sometimes, non-Christians are troubled by accusing thoughts, for this reason. At other times, they think of excuses, but deep in their hearts they know they have done wrong and deserve to be punished.

The Jewish people guilty before God (2:17–3:18)

Paul now turns his attention to the Jewish people, the Old Testament people of God. They thought they were justified before God and superior to others because they knew about the law (2:17–20). However, they were wrong, because they did not practise what they preached (2:21–22) and, as a result, God was dishonoured (2:23–24). Paul charges them with stealing and adultery, contrary to the Ten Commandments. Also, although the Jewish people claimed to hate idolatry, they were not above robbing temples and profiting from the sale of the stolen idols!

In Old Testament times, circumcision was the outward sign that a man belonged to the people of God. However, outward signs are worth nothing if it makes no difference to how we behave (2:25–29). This applies equally to Christian baptism nowadays. Outward ceremonies have their place, but they are not a condition of salvation and they are worth nothing apart from the inward change produced by the gospel.

This prompts the question asked in chapter 3:1: 'What advantage then has the Jew, or what is the profit of circumcision?' Answer: there are many advantages, but the main one is having the Holy Scriptures (3:2). The fact that 'some did not believe' did not nullify the reliability of God's Word and the advantage of having it (3:3). Men may lie, but God does not (3:4; see also Numbers 23:19). The Bible is the truth, the whole truth, and nothing but the truth, and having it is a great advantage. (The Old Testament quotation in 3:4 comes from the ancient Greek *Septuagint* version of Psalm 51:4. Paul's use of the Septuagint explains why quotations from the Old Testament do not always match what we have in our English Old Testament.)

> The Bible is the truth, the whole truth, and nothing but the truth, and having it is a great advantage.

In Romans 3:5, Paul asks another question: 'Is God unjust who inflicts wrath?' The contrast between the lies and unrighteousness of men and the truth and righteousness of God makes the latter shine even brighter. However, this does not make it wrong for God to punish sin. 'Certainly not!', says Paul. God is going to judge the world, and this inevitably involves punishing sin (3:6). Nor does the fact that our lies and unrighteousness make the truth and righteousness of God shine even brighter justify lies and unrighteousness. Some people wickedly perverted Paul's teaching to affirm this, but 'their condemnation is just', says the apostle (3:7–8).

Ever since 1:18, Paul has been showing us why the gospel is needed. He has looked at the pagan world, then dominated by Greek culture but rejecting the truth about God and sunk in a degraded lifestyle; he has looked at the Jewish people who knew better but did not practise what they preached; he has explained the main advantage of being a Jew; and he has said that it is right and proper for God to judge the world and punish sin. Now comes the summing up. The Jews are no better than the Gentiles—'they are all under sin' (3:9). Among all the offspring of Adam, there is not even one whose behaviour is righteous (3:10). There is not even one who understands, *or even wants to understand*, the truth about God (3:11). 'They have all turned aside; they have together become unprofitable; there is none who does good, *no, not one*' (3:12).

Paul's authority for saying these things is the Bible, the Holy Scriptures. Verses 10–12 are quotations from the Old Testament (Psalm 14:1–3 and Psalm 53:1–3) and so are verses 13–18 (Psalm 5:9; Psalm 140:3; Psalm 10:7; Isaiah 59:7–8; Psalm 36:1). The latter verses give us a picture of what sin is like. It affects our words (3:13–14), our ways (3:15–17) and our worship (3:18). We are not as bad as we possibly could be, but every part of our being is affected by sin.

The whole world guilty before God (3:19–20)

Verses 10–18 are primarily addressed to the Jewish people (3:19a), but this is so that 'every mouth may be stopped, and all the world may become guilty before God' (3:19b). If even the Jewish people with all their advantages are sinners, then there are no exceptions—no one has a viable defence; the verdict must be guilty! The law of God is not a way of salvation, but a mirror to show us our sin (3:20).

FOR FURTHER STUDY

1. Paul says that the wrath of God has been revealed to some extent even now. Look at Genesis 3:9–24; 6:5–8; and 18:20–33 to consider examples of this.

TO THINK ABOUT AND DISCUSS

1. Human anger is often (though not always) sinful, whereas the anger of God is always righteous. In our preaching of the gospel, what should we say to safeguard this truth from being misunderstood?

3 Justification by faith

(3:21–4:25)

We have now come to the very heart of Romans. This is where we come to understand that the price has been paid and God's justice has been satisfied for everyone who trusts in the Lord Jesus Christ as their Saviour. This teaching should warm our hearts and transform our lives.

Justification by faith explained (3:21–26)

This section begins with the words, 'But now' (3:21a). The storm clouds of God's wrath were looming over us (1:18, 2:5, 2:8 and 3:5), *but now* the sun is shining and there is a lovely rainbow. Something has happened in history to change everything. The apostle says, 'the righteousness of God apart from the law is revealed' (3:21a)—not the righteousness of God in punishing sinners, but in justifying them (i.e. declaring them righteous or *not guilty*), because justice was satisfied at Calvary's Cross. Understanding this was the key that unlocked Romans for Dr Martin Luther, so that it became to him the gate of heaven.

This way of salvation is totally 'apart from the law'—it has nothing to do with us doing what the law says we should do. Justification is 'by faith apart from the deeds of the law' (3:28). However, it was witnessed by 'the Law and the Prophets' (3:21b). The Old Testament prophets looked forward to the coming of 'Messiah the Prince' (Daniel 9:25), and the whole Old Testament can be viewed as a preparation for His coming. The giving of the law at Mount Sinai was to make us feel our need of a Saviour, as we have already seen (3:20); the Old Testament sacrificial system pointed forward to the Lord's one great sacrifice at Calvary's Cross (Hebrews 10:11–12); and even as far back as Abraham in the book of Genesis, we find that 'the Scripture, foreseeing that God would justify the Gentiles by faith, preached the gospel to Abraham beforehand' (Galatians 3:8).

The righteousness of God in justifying sinners is given to us when we put our trust in Jesus Christ (3:22a). It is offered to all mankind, but it only benefits us when we believe and trust in Him as our Saviour (3:22a). This righteousness is like a robe that covers us before God (see Isaiah 61:10).

But how can it be right to offer salvation to all, regardless of what they have done? Answer: 'there is no difference; for all have sinned and fall short of the glory of God' (3:22b–23). Some may be worse than others, but we are all guilty sinners who fall far short of what is required to enter heaven and share in the glory of God. We all need to be 'justified freely by His grace' (3:24a), that is, by His free, unmerited favour.

OK, that is what we need, but is it right? Should we not all be sent to hell? No. Justification can be freely offered to all because it is 'through the redemption that is in Christ Jesus' (3:24b). *To redeem* means 'to buy back' and Paul is saying that the Lord Jesus Christ has paid the great price of salvation in full on our behalf. God is right to justify sinners because His justice, His righteous anger against sin, was fully satisfied at Calvary's Cross where Christ Jesus our Saviour was set forth 'as a propitiation by His blood, through faith, to demonstrate His righteousness' (3:25a). This includes the sins of Old Testament believers, 'the sins that were previously committed', and it includes the sins of believers 'at the present time' as well (3:25b–26).

> God is right to justify sinners because His justice, His righteous anger against sin, was fully satisfied at Calvary's Cross.

The Greek word translated as 'propitiation' or 'sacrifice of atonement' (NIV) is the same word that is used by the Septuagint (the ancient Greek translation of the Old Testament) to refer to 'the mercy seat'. On the

Day of Atonement, a goat was killed as a 'sin offering ... for the people' and some of the blood was sprinkled 'on the mercy seat and before the mercy seat' (Leviticus 16:15–17). Thus, at-one-ment was made, but only as a foreshadowing of the Lord Jesus Christ's one great sacrifice at Calvary's Cross.

He has made a full atonement,

Now His saving work is done;

He has satisfied the Father,

Who accepts us in His Son.

(Maud Frazer Jackson, 1873–1950)

It is now clear that God can be 'just and the Justifier of the one who has faith in Jesus' (3:26b). Justification is more than forgiveness. It means being declared righteous or not guilty in respect of all those things that could be charged against us (see 8:33). It is *just as if I'd never sinned*. The price has been paid! God's justice has been satisfied! The whole world is guilty before God according to the law of Moses, but thank God, those who have faith in Jesus are 'justified from all things' (see Acts 13:38–39).

Three important questions (3:27–31)

Returning to Romans, Paul now asks three important questions to see whether we have understood his teaching:

'Where is boasting then?' (3:27) The 'law' or principle of works allows for boasting, but the principle of faith excludes it (Ephesians 2:8–9). We come to God confessing that we are sinners and that we have nothing to boast about, and we put our trust simply and solely in the Lord Jesus Christ as our Saviour. Works are excluded and we have the wonderful conclusion that 'a man is justified by faith apart from the deeds of the law' (3:28).

'Is ... [God] the God of the Jews only? Is He not also the God of the Gentiles?' (3:29a). To start with, the early Christians were all Jewish and some thought that, as well as trusting in the Lord Jesus Christ, male Gentiles needed to be circumcised (Acts 15:1). However, the teaching of justification by faith negates that. Circumcised Jews still need faith and uncircumcised Gentiles only need faith. There is one God and one way to God (3:29b–30).

'Do we then make void the law through faith?' (3:31a). 'Certainly not!', says Paul, 'On the contrary, we establish the law' (3:31b). We establish the law in its right use by acknowledging our sin and guilt (see 3:19–20). Also, the Lord Jesus Christ established the law by enduring its penalty, which is death, on our behalf. The law says, 'The soul who sins shall die' (Ezekiel 18:20a), but our Lord died *for us*. He did not bypass the law. Instead, He endured its penalty on our behalf.

Justification by faith illustrated by the life of Abraham (4:1–25)

Having set forth the doctrine of justification by faith and

tested whether we understand it, the apostle now refers to Abraham and David, the two most important men in the Old Testament (see Matthew 1:1). The Scripture definitely says that Abraham's faith was 'accounted to him [or put to his account] for righteousness' (4:1–3; Genesis 15:6), and 'David also describes the blessedness of the man to whom God imputes [or puts to his account] righteousness apart from works' (4:6). In both cases, Paul is talking about righteousness being put to someone's account. This is what happens when we are justified by faith. Our sins were put to the account of the Lord Jesus Christ (see Isaiah 53:6). He satisfied justice by dying for them and what He accomplished is put to our account, when we put our trust in Him.

The fact that Abraham's faith was 'accounted to him for righteousness' makes it clear that he was not justified by works (see 4:4–5) and David's Psalm likewise excludes works (4:6–8; Psalm 32:1–2). However, there is still the possibility that the Old Testament might limit the blessing of being justified by faith to those who were circumcised. The apostle deals with this final objection by pointing out that Abraham had righteousness put to his account *before* he was circumcised (see 4:9–10). This was so that he could be 'the father of all those who believe', whether circumcised or not (see 4:11–12).

God promised Abraham 'that he would be the heir of the world' (4:13a)—in him all nations would be blessed (see Genesis 12:3 and 22:18). This promise has been and will be fulfilled in the Lord Jesus Christ (see Galatians 3:16). *He* is the Heir of the world and Christians are 'joint heirs' with Him (8:16–17a). The promise 'was not ... through the law' (4:13). It was made to Abraham 430 years before the law was given to Israel (Galatians 3:17).

If it were through the law, the fulfilment of the promise would depend upon our trying to keep the law, and failure to do so would render the promise ineffective (4:14). The law brings not blessing but the righteous anger of God upon sinners (4:15a; Galatians 3:10), but 'where there is no law there is no transgression' (4:15b). If the law is removed from the equation and if 'it is of faith that it might be according to grace', then the promise is 'sure' to all the believing children of Abraham (4:16).

The God in whom Abraham believed, 'gives life to the dead' and calls things into existence by His Word (4:17; Genesis 1:3, 6, 9, 11, etc.) When God said 'I have made you a father of many nations', Abraham was ninety-nine years old and Isaac did not exist (see Genesis 17:5), but Abraham believed what God said (4:18; Genesis 15:5). In spite of the seeming impossibility, Abraham's faith gave 'glory to God' (4:19–20). He was 'fully convinced that what ... [God] had promised He was also able to perform' (4:21). This is why Abraham's faith in what God had promised was the channel by means of which righteousness was put to his account (4:22). As we saw at the end of chapter 3, the principle of faith excludes boasting and gives glory to God (see 3:27–28).

This is the pattern for us as well (4:23–24). Just as Abraham believed in God, who gives life to the dead, even so must we. Saving faith in the Lord Jesus Christ trusts in the promise of God, smiles at impossibilities and says, 'It shall be done!'. The Lord Jesus 'was delivered up *because of* our offenses, and was raised *because of* our justification' (4:25)—the Cross is the proof of our sinfulness and the

> Saving faith in the Lord Jesus Christ trusts in the promise of God, smiles at impossibilities and says, 'It shall be done!'.

Resurrection is the proof of our justification. 'The wages of sin [even one sin] is death' (6:23a; see also Genesis 2:16–17). Therefore, the fact that the Lord Jesus Christ rose again proves that every sin has been paid for and no charge will ever be brought against those who trust in Him. Hallelujah!

For further study ▶

FOR FURTHER STUDY

1. Paul says that justification by faith was 'witnessed by the Law and the Prophets' (3:21). Look at Genesis 15:1–6; Psalm 32; and Habakkuk 2:1–4 to find examples of this.

2. Paul illustrates his teaching by the life of Abraham. Look at Hebrews 11:8–19 which also focuses on the vital impact of faith on his life.

TO THINK ABOUT AND DISCUSS

1. Saving faith is more than just believing that certain things are true. It also includes trusting in God and the Lord Jesus Christ as our Saviour. How is this illustrated in the life of Abraham?

4 Justification by faith at the Reformation and later

Paul's epistle to the Romans and especially the doctrine of justification of faith has been of very great importance in church history. This chapter tells the story of the conversion of Martin Luther and also how the same great truth proved equally important hundreds of years later.

A young man decided to become a monk. He entered the Augustinian cloister at Erfurt in Germany on 17th July 1505, at the age of twenty-one. Martin Luther was afraid to die and he thought this was the best way to obtain the salvation of his immortal soul.

Luther entered into the discipline of the monastic way of life wholeheartedly. He himself said, 'If I had kept on any longer, I should have killed myself with vigils, prayers, reading and other work'. However, these things failed to give him any sense of inner tranquillity.

Providentially, Dr Staupitz, the head of the Augustinian order, gave Luther a new focus by appointing him the professor of the Bible at the newly founded Wittenberg University. On 16th August 1513, Luther's lectures on The Psalms began. Then, in April 1515, he switched to giving lectures on the apostle Paul's epistle to the Romans.

These studies in Romans were the Damascus Road for Martin Luther. Let us hear the story in his own words:

I greatly longed to understand Paul's epistle to the Romans and nothing stood in the way but that one expression, 'the justice [or righteousness] of God,' because I took it to mean that justice whereby God is just and deals justly in punishing the unjust. My situation was that, although an impeccable monk, I stood before God as a sinner troubled in conscience, and I had no confidence that my merit would assuage Him. Therefore, I did not love a just and angry God,

> 'Although an impeccable monk, I stood before God as a sinner troubled in conscience, and I had no confidence that my merit would assuage Him.'

but rather hated and murmured against Him. Yet I clung to the dear Paul and had a great yearning to know what he meant.

Night and day, I pondered until I saw the connection between the justice of God and the statement that 'the just shall live by his faith'. Then I grasped that the justice of God is that righteousness by which through grace and sheer mercy God justifies us through faith. Thereupon I felt myself to be reborn and to have gone through open doors into Paradise. The whole of Scripture took on a new meaning, and whereas before the 'justice of God' had filled me with hate, now it became to me inexpressibly sweet in greater love. This passage of Paul became to me a gate to heaven ...

If you have a true faith that Christ is your Saviour, then at once you have a gracious God, for faith leads you in and opens up God's heart and will, that you should see pure grace and overflowing love. This it is to behold God in faith that you should look upon His fatherly, friendly heart, in which there is no anger nor ungraciousness ... [1]

Thus, the serious study of Romans first transformed Martin Luther's own heart and life and then caused him to rise up and shake the whole of Europe!

One of the places that was greatly affected by the Protestant Reformation was the city of Geneva. This was where the great John Calvin preached and exerted so much influence from 1541 until his death in 1564. However, if we fast forward 252 years to 1816, we find that things were very different. The light of the gospel was no longer shining brightly.

Then a Scotsman named Robert Haldane happened to visit Geneva. Dr Martyn Lloyd-Jones, the famous Welsh preacher, says:

As if by accident, he came into contact with a number of students who were studying for the ministry. They were all blind to spiritual truth but felt much attracted to Haldane and to what he said. He arranged, therefore, that they should come regularly twice a week to the rooms where he was staying and he took them through and expounded to them Paul's epistle to the Romans. One by one they were converted, and their conversion led to a true revival of religion, not only in Switzerland, but also in France ... It was at the request of such men that Robert Haldane decided to put into print what he had been telling them.

Haldane's great commentary is still available today with a foreword by Dr Lloyd-Jones from which I have quoted.[2] Dr Lloyd-Jones says that 'one cannot read it without being conscious of the preacher as well as the expositor.'

Finally, let us fast forward another 120 years or so and cross over the Atlantic Ocean to the United States. Here we find that the light of the gospel was still shining brightly in many places, but side-by-side with this, the destructive effect of liberal theology was undermining the Christian faith in many theological colleges. Dr Harry Ironside, the pastor for eighteen years of Chicago's famous Moody Memorial Church, tells about 'a dear young man who came to me not long ago in a nearby city. He said, "Do you recognize me?" I looked at him and said, "I'm afraid I don't. Your face looks somewhat familiar ... but I can't recall your name." "Well," he said, "I couldn't forget you because God used you to help me when I needed it, oh so badly."' Let us hear the young man tell his story in his own words:

I had gone as a young man to a certain seminary. I went in as an earnest, flaming evangelist, and after four years in cold storage there I came out practically an agnostic. They had filled me with doubt and perplexity. They told me the Bible was not the inspired Word of God. They told me that blood atonement was not the way sinners were saved, and I came out of there with nothing to preach. I did not know where I stood myself. I thought I would go into business or take up some other profession. I was passing through Chicago, and my train connection left me some hours to look around. I had heard of the Moody Church, so I thought I would go up there ... you [Dr Ironside] took me through the building and then up into your study. I told you how confused I was and you sought to help me, and prayed with me, and just as I was leaving you handed me your book on the Epistle to the Romans[3] [still available today as Romans and Galatians, published by Kregel Publications]. I read it on the train; and by the time I got home, all my doubts were gone, and I had a gospel to preach again. That book changed my life, and for eight years I have been preaching the gospel in a Methodist church and winning many souls to Christ.[4]

This time, the study of Romans was used to deliver a Christian young man from doubt and perplexity, leading on to the winning of 'many souls to Christ'. Dr Ironside's *Lectures on the Epistle to the Romans* consists of eleven lectures which cover the whole epistle. The lectures were given to the students at the Moody Bible Institute of Chicago, the Dallas Theological Seminary and at various Bible conferences. I myself have found them most helpful.

'FOR FURTHER STUDY'

1. Read a good biography of the life of Martin Luther. For example, Here I Stand: A Life of Martin Luther by Professor Roland Bainton, (Hendrickson Publishers, 2012).

TO THINK ABOUT AND DISCUSS

1. Why is it important to know about church history?

5 Consequences and an explanation

(5:1–21)

In this study we find that not only is justification by faith wonderful in itself, but it has wonderful consequences as well. Also, the apostle gives us an explanation for the universality of sin.

The consequences of justification by faith (5:1–11)

I n our third study, we saw the storm clouds of God's wrath being dissipated by the sunshine of God's grace. Because of what was accomplished at Calvary's Cross, God is 'the Justifier of the one who has faith in Jesus' (3:26). Truly, Romans is a gate to heaven for whoever is willing to put their trust in Him.

It is indeed a wonderful thing that God is 'the Justifier of the one who has faith in Jesus' (3:26), and it has wonderful consequences too. The seven consequences of justification by faith are as follows:

1. 'PEACE [OR FRIENDSHIP] WITH GOD' (5:1)
Justice has been satisfied and friendly relations between God and mankind are now possible. God invites us to

enter into friendship with Him by trusting in the Lord Jesus Christ. This is what the apostle Paul refers to as the 'ministry of reconciliation' (2 Corinthians 5:18–20). What a wonderful thing it is that God is not only our Creator and our Saviour, but also our Friend!

This is only possible 'through our Lord Jesus Christ' (5:1). He is the one and only way by which lost sinners can come back to God the Father (John 14:6). This is because He is the only One who was able to die to atone for our sins (1 Timothy 2:5–6; 1 Peter 3:18a).

In one of his hymns, the great hymnwriter, Horatius Bonar (1808–89), referred to peace with God as 'this blood-sealed friendship'. That is what it is. It is worth more than the whole world and everything in it. This is why Christians are rightly exhorted to 'be content with such things as you have' (Hebrews 13:5). God is our Friend who has promised never to leave us nor forsake us. We ought to be content!

2. 'ACCESS … INTO THIS GRACE IN WHICH WE STAND' (5:2A)

Having been justified by faith, we have access to the resources of God's grace. In Old Testament times, when people approached God, they came first to the altar of burnt offering. This foreshadowed Calvary's Cross where the Lord Jesus Christ obtained justification and peace with God for us. Then, after coming to the altar of burnt offering, they came to the laver, the lampstand, the table of showbread, the altar of incense and 'the Most Holy Place' (Hebrews 9:3, NIV). These things foreshadowed the resources of God's grace to which Christians have access—daily cleansing from sin, the light of God's Word, spiritual nourishment, the privilege of prayer and fellowship with God Himself.

3. 'HOPE OF THE GLORY OF GOD' (5:2B)

'All have sinned and fall short of the glory of God' (3:23), but the wonderful thing is that Christians 'rejoice in hope of the glory of God'. We look forward to entering heaven and sharing in the glory of God. We are told in chapter 8 that 'whom He justified, these He also glorified' (8:30b). This is the 'sure and steadfast' hope in which we rejoice, through our Lord Jesus Christ. He has already 'entered [heaven] for us', 'to prepare a place for [us] ...' and to intercede for us until one day we arrive safely at our heavenly home (Hebrews 6:19–20; John 14:2–3).

Therefore, because we have been declared righteous by trusting in the Lord Jesus Christ as our Saviour, these things follow *now*: friendship with God; access to the resources of God's grace; and an exultant hope of heaven and glory. However, as regards actually entering heaven, the bitter must come before the sweet ...

4. 'TRIBULATIONS' (5:3–4)

The Bible says that Christians must expect to pass

'through many tribulations' on their way to heaven (Acts 14:22). However, it is more than that. Paul says we '*glory* [or *rejoice*] in tribulations' (5:3a) just as we 'rejoice in hope' (5:2)! It is the same word in the Greek. However, we do not always find this easy! We groan in tribulations and wish they would stop, but the clue to what Paul means is the next word—'knowing'. We understand that tough times have a good purpose—they are an opportunity for Christians to prove the genuineness of their faith and they can lead to an even greater hope and assurance. I believe this is the meaning of 5:3b–4.

As regards 'character' (5:4), I think 'experience' (KJV) or 'approvedness' (ASV) are better translations. It is by persevering through difficult times 'that the Christian approves himself and shows that he is no fair-weather professor'.[1] See the great promise in Isaiah 43:1–2 which says, 'When you pass through the waters, I will be with you; and through the rivers, they shall not overflow you.'

> We understand that tough times have a good purpose.

When through the deep waters I cause thee to go,

The rivers of woe shall not thee overflow;

For I will be with thee, thy troubles to bless,

And sanctify to thee thy deepest distress.

(John Rippon's *Selection of Hymns*, 1787)

5. 'The love of God ... poured out in our hearts' (5:5–8)

The exultant hope, that Christians can and should have, is corroborated by the Holy Spirit who causes us to know and feel the greatness of God's love for us (5:5). This is what Paul prayed for the Ephesians in Ephesians 3:16–19. Returning to Romans, it is God's love for us that is in view. This is clear from the next three verses. The greatness of this love is shown by the fact that the Lord Jesus Christ 'died for the ungodly' (5:6)—those who do not give God His rightful place in their lives and deserve nothing from Him. The highest human love is to die for the deserving (5:7), but God's love is for sinners (5:8). May the Holy Spirit indeed cause us to know and feel the greatness of God's love for us!

God commends His love—

Greater could not be:

While I was a sinner,

Jesus died for me.

(George Goodman, 1866–1942)

6. 'We shall be saved' (5:9–10)

In one sense, Christians 'have been saved' already. Paul says this in Ephesians 2:8–9. Already, we have been justified before God and reconciled to Him by the death—by the shed blood—of His Son, the Lord Jesus Christ. Therefore, we do not need to fear 'the day of wrath' (2:5). On that day, 'we *shall be saved* from wrath through Him' (5:9). The argument is from the greater to the lesser. Look at verse 10. This is saying that because God has done the greater thing of reconciling enemies, we can be sure that He will do the lesser thing of saving friends. The expression, 'by His life', refers to our Lord's resurrection life. It means that because 'He always lives to make intercession for [us] ...' (Hebrews 7:25) and because He is coming again to give us glorious resurrection bodies (Philippians 3:20–21), we can be sure that one day all the benefits of salvation will be ours, if we are trusting in Jesus as our Saviour.

7. 'WE ALSO REJOICE IN GOD' (5:11)

We rejoice in our salvation, but it goes beyond that. We rejoice *in God*; we rejoice in the One who has saved us. This is what the Old Testament prophet Habakkuk did. He said, 'I will rejoice in the LORD, I will joy in the God of my salvation' (Habakkuk 3:18). God is no longer a terror to us, but our best Friend. We 'rejoice in God through our Lord Jesus Christ, through whom we have *now* received the reconciliation [the friendship with God]'. Do you see that word '*now*'? This friendship with God is our present possession.

> From Him who loves me *now* so well
>
> What power my soul can sever?
>
> Shall life or death, or earth or hell?
>
> No! I am His for ever.
>
> (James Grindlay Small, 1817–88)

An explanation (5:12–21)

So far in Romans we have seen three main things:

1. The whole world is guilty before God because of sin.
2. Because of the Cross, the sinner can be justified by faith in Jesus.
3. There are wonderful consequences.

It is indeed wonderful to know that, by trusting in Jesus as our Saviour, our sins are forgiven and we have a righteous standing before God. We are so grateful to our Saviour and we love Him very much. We desire to follow Him. However, the new Christian soon discovers that we have an old sinful nature still dwelling within us. The Christian life is a struggle and we are often defeated, but the good news is that there is a way of victory. In my view, the main things Paul addresses from the start of chapter 6 until the end of chapter 8 are this struggle and the ultimate triumph of grace. Romans 5:12–21 provides an explanation for the universality of sin and lays a foundation for what follows.

> The Christian life is a struggle and we are often defeated, but the good news is that there is a way of victory.

Paul begins this part of Romans by going right back to Adam. He clearly believed that Adam was a historical figure. Indeed, the historicity of the first eleven chapters of Genesis is never questioned in the entire New Testament. (I recommend any reader who is concerned about this subject to read Professor Andy McIntosh's commentary *Genesis 1–11*.)[2]

When God made the world, the Bible says that 'it was very good' (Genesis 1:31). There was no sin and no death. This would have continued to be the case if Adam had obeyed God's commandment, but he did not. Sin and death entered the world and affected all mankind (5:12). Theologians call this 'the Fall'. Four ages or distinct periods of time in the history of mankind can be distinguished by reference to the Fall, the giving of the law, and the Cross, as follows:

- The Age of Innocence: the time before the Fall
- The Age of Conscience: the time from the Fall to the giving of the law
- The Age of Law: the time from the giving of the law to the Cross
- The Age of Grace or the Gospel Age: the time from the Cross to the Second Coming

During the Age of Conscience, 'sin was in the world' (5:13a) and 'death reigned' (5:14a). However, there was no law, no clearly stated Ten Commandments. Mankind had only the light of creation and conscience. Nevertheless, sin was in the world and death reigned, but the sins they committed were, in the main, not 'according to the likeness of the transgression of Adam'

(5:14). You see, Adam *did* sin against a clearly stated commandment (see Genesis 2:16–17) and it was this sin that caused many to die. Paul says, 'By the one man's offense many died' (5:15a). This is because Adam was the head of mankind and his one act had implications for the whole race. In this respect, he foreshadowed the Lord Jesus Christ, who is the Head of a new race and whose one act of obedience at Calvary's Cross has implications for all who trust in Him (5:15–19). I have set this out in tabular form:

Figure 1	ADAM	CHRIST
One Act	The Fall	The Cross
Scope	Universal	Sufficient for all; effective for all who believe
Implications	Condemnation Death	Justification Life

So, both Adam and the Lord Jesus Christ did one thing that was potentially universal in scope, but the implications are in sharp contrast. Also, there is something 'much more' about what the Lord Jesus did (5:15, 17). 'In Him the tribes of Adam boast more blessings than their father lost', says Isaac Watts (1674–1748), the hymnwriter. Much more!

There is another 'much more' in verse 20, to do with the Age of Law and the Age of Grace. Paul says, 'the law entered that the offense might abound' (5:20a). It sounds strange, but this is what the law does—it stirs up sin, just as a 'keep off' or 'do not touch' notice incites us to do the opposite. However, this does not mean that there is anything wrong with the law—it is like a sterling silver spoon. Imagine a glass of clear water (representing our apparently respectable, decent and law-abiding lives) with dirt at the bottom (representing our sinful passions). Then, take the spoon and stir it. The water now looks horrible, but this is not the fault of the spoon! It is simply showing what was there all the time. Likewise, the law showed how bad mankind's sin problem was.

However, the Age of Law ended at the Cross and now it is the Age of Grace—abounding grace that is 'much more' than a match for stirred-up sin (5:20b). Of course, salvation has always been by grace throughout all the ages of history, but now grace reigns. It is on the throne, because the One who died for us is on the throne (5:21).

Marvellous grace of our loving Lord,

Grace that exceeds our sin and our guilt,

Yonder on Calvary's mount outpoured,

There where the blood of the Lamb was spilt.

(Julia H. Johnston, 1849–1919)

For further study ▶

'FOR FURTHER STUDY'

1. One of the consequences of justification by faith is peace with or reconciliation to God. Look at 2 Corinthians 5:18–21 to see how this is a vital part of the preaching of the gospel.

2. Paul's explanation of the universality of sin is based on a literal Adam. Likewise, the Lord Jesus Christ spoke about a literal creation of mankind, a literal Noah and the Flood, and a literal Lot and the destruction of Sodom and Gomorrah. Look at Matthew 19:3–6 and Luke 17:26–32.

TO THINK ABOUT AND DISCUSS

1. What is the difference between peace with God and 'the peace of God' which Paul speaks about in Philippians 4:6–7?

2. Is one reason why people refuse to listen to the gospel because they have been misled into thinking that science has disproved the historicity of the early chapters of Genesis? If so, how should we go about overcoming this barrier?

6 The struggle

(6:1 – 8:2)

It is wonderful that, by trusting in Jesus as our Saviour, our sins are forgiven and we have a righteous standing before God. We desire to follow Him. However, the new Christian soon discovers that we have an old sinful nature still dwelling within us. The Christian life is a struggle, but the good news is that there is a way of victory.

The tyranny of sin is over (6:1 – 14)

I concluded the previous study by saying that we are now living in the Age of Grace. Grace reigns! It is on the throne! However, when non-Christians hear about salvation being by grace through faith, some conclude that our behaviour does not matter and that we can 'continue in sin' (6:1). 'Certainly not!' says Paul, and so says every true believer (6:2a). The thing is, 'faith [works] through love' (Galatians 5:6b)—it is not a case of *having* to do what is right but *wanting to*. Moreover, continuing in sin is inconsistent with having 'died to sin' (6:2b). What this means is explained in the next few verses.

Paul speaks first about baptism (6:3). Baptism is commanded as a public testimony to our faith and as a *sign* of grace, but it does not *confer* grace. We are justified before God the moment we truly trust in the Lord Jesus Christ as our Saviour.

The reason Paul mentions baptism is because baptism by immersion is a good illustration of our union with the Lord Jesus Christ in death and resurrection. The apostle says that, because of this union, 'we also should walk in newness of life' (6:4). This is the *new life in Christ* implied by that grand watchword of the Protestant Reformation, 'The just shall live by faith' (1:17b).

We need to follow the apostle's argument carefully. He says, in the next few verses, that there are certain things we need to 'know' or understand:

- 'Knowing this ... that we should no longer be slaves of sin' (6:6). We need to understand that the Lord Jesus died and rose again, not only so that our sins can be forgiven, but also so that we can be set free from the tyranny of sin.

- 'Knowing that Christ, having been raised from the dead, dies no more ...' (6:9–10). We also need to understand that the Lord Jesus Christ is never going to die again. Sin no longer has any claim on Him (He was the utterly sinless One who died to atone for *our* sins)—He has died 'to sin once for all', and now 'He lives to God' (6:10).

Now, the point of all this is that Christians are to reckon that all this is true of themselves, because of our union with the Lord in death and resurrection (6:11). Sin no longer has any legitimate claim on us and we can give our lives wholly to God (6:12–13). Yes, we are conscious of the fact that our old sinful nature still dwells within us, but, by the grace of God, we do not need to give way to it (6:14). Grace produces what the law demands, by first justifying us and then enabling us to live a new life.

Sin shall not have dominion over you,

Oh, what a glorious message, and it's true,

God has said it, it must stand,

Pass it on, it's simply grand,

Sin shall *not* have dominion over you.

(R. Hudson Pope, 1879–1967)

Who do we want to serve? (6:15–19)

In the next verse, Paul again squashes the idea that our behaviour does not matter (6:15). People who say this do not understand grace. You see, grace puts a new 'want to' in our hearts. The implied question in the next few verses is, 'Who do we want to serve—sin or God?' If we give way to our old sinful nature, then we are to some extent serving sin (6:16). Certainly, this was true before we became Christians, but thanks be to God, a change has taken place—we have 'obeyed from the heart' the gospel doctrine by trusting in the Lord Jesus Christ (6:17). By this first step of obedience, we are set free from the claims of sin and constituted 'slaves [or servants] of righteousness' (6:18). However, even though the heart is obedient, the flesh is weak and giving way to our old sinful nature is still possible—Paul speaks about 'the weakness of your flesh' (6:19a; see also Matthew 26:41). We need to be careful and prayerful to give every part of our lives to holiness and to God (6:19).

Which service is better? (6:20–23)

The next implied question is: 'Which service is better?' The service of sin does not produce anything worthwhile; it is shameful and it ends in death (6:21). By contrast, the service of God is very worthwhile; it is holy and it ends in everlasting life (6:22). We have a foretaste of everlasting life even now—we can walk in newness of life even now—but the fullness awaits the life to come. So then, one end is death, the other is everlasting life. One end is well-deserved, the other is the gracious 'gift of God' which is offered to us 'in Christ Jesus our Lord' (6:23). The bottom line is this. Genuine Christians know that they want to serve this gracious God who has given us eternal life in His Son, Jesus Christ (see 1 John 5:11–12).

Christians are dead to the law (7:1–6)

We have seen that Christians are dead to sin in chapter 6 and now, here in chapter 7, we discover that Christians are 'dead to the law' as well (see 7:4a). Neither sin nor the law has any legitimate claim upon us because of Calvary's Cross. I believe the meaning of the first four verses is that the law was our old 'husband' (strange though that may sound!), but death, the death of the Lord Jesus Christ on our behalf, has ended the relationship. 'Therefore', says Paul, 'you also have become dead to the law through the body of Christ' (7:4a). We find the same teaching in his epistle to the Galatians (see Galatians 2:19–20). The death of the Lord Jesus has ended our relationship to the law.

> Even though the heart is obedient, the flesh is weak and giving way to our old sinful nature is still possible.

The law was a demanding husband, but the only thing it succeeded in doing was to stir up our 'sinful passions ... to bear fruit to death' (7:5). However, this does not mean that we are free to sin. Perish the thought! The old relationship has ended and now we are free to 'serve in the newness of the Spirit and not in the oldness of the letter' (7:6). We are 'married to another—to Him who was raised from the dead' (7:4b). This is a 'marriage' based on love and the result is 'fruit to God' (7:4b).

There is nothing wrong with the law (7:7–12)

The preceding remarks do not mean that there is

anything wrong with the law. It is God's law. The Ten Commandments provide a perfect basis for the law of any land. However, the law of God was never intended to be a way of salvation. Rather, its purpose is to show us our sin (7:7a). The tenth commandment is a good example (7:7b). Sin seemed to be dead in Saul the Pharisee, but when the tenth commandment came home to him, he realised that sin is not only an outward deed, but also an inward desire. The law stirred up these desires, sin came to life and Paul realised that he had a sinful nature and that the law condemned him to death (7:8–9).

The apostle says, 'the commandment, which was to bring life, I found to bring death' (7:10), but the commandment was not to blame. The problem was that 'sin, taking occasion by the commandment, deceived me' (7:11a). When we are tempted to break God's commandments, we can think we are going to get something good, to live life to the full, but it is not true! Sin leads to death, not life. 'Sin … killed me', says Paul (7:11). So then, there is nothing wrong with the law. It is 'holy and just and good', as the next verse says (7:12).

The struggle with sin (7:13–25)

There is nothing wrong with the law. This is the problem: there is something wrong *with us*. We have a sinful nature. The purpose of the law is to show us our sin—this is the meaning of the next two verses (7:13–14).

Now, let us remember the big picture. If we are trusting in the Lord Jesus Christ as our Saviour, then our sins have been forgiven and we have a righteous standing before God. We are justified by faith. However, this is the remaining problem: although we genuinely want to follow the Lord Jesus Christ, we still have a sinful nature. This is emphasised in the next few verses. As born-again believers, we hate sin and yet we often commit sin (7:15). '[We] agree with the law that it is good', but there is an enemy within (7:16–18a). We want to do good, but we fail (7:18b). We do evil instead (7:19). This is not the fault of the new nature—the new 'want to' that grace puts in our hearts. It is the fault of the old nature—what Paul calls 'sin that dwells in me' (7:20). This old nature, this indwelling sin, is an adverse 'law' or principle at work within us (7:21). The law of God, the law given through Moses, cannot help us, even though it is 'holy and just and good' and we delight in it 'according to the inward man' (7:22).

Some people suggest that in this chapter Paul is speaking as if he were a non-Christian. They quote the saying of the pagan Roman poet Ovid, 'I see what is better and approve of it; I follow what is worse'[1], and suggest that Paul is saying the same thing. I do not agree. I do not believe that a non-Christian ever 'delight[s] in the law of God according to the inward man' (7:22). Also, what Paul is doing in chapters 6–8 is to speak about the struggle which every Christian does experience and to show that the gospel has an answer. Therefore, to suggest that in this chapter Paul is speaking as if he were a non-Christian is totally out of place, in my opinion.

So, returning to the apostle's argument, he says there are two 'laws', or principles, at work in the Christian. The 'law of my mind' is the desire that every born-again believer has to follow God's way, but there is also 'the law of sin which is in my members' (7:23). Paul says he can see it 'warring against the law of my mind, and bringing me into captivity'. The old sinful nature that dwells within us is like the law of gravity: it pulls us down. It is impossible to overcome this downward pull unaided and so the Christian cries out for deliverance (7:24). Thank God, there is a way of victory 'through Jesus Christ our Lord (7:25a)! However, this is the subject of the next section. The conclusion of this section is that, although born-again believers want to serve the law of God, the sinful nature pulls us down (7:25b).

> Although we genuinely want to follow the Lord Jesus Christ, we still have a sinful nature.

The way of victory (8:1–2)

Paul has spoken about two principles—'the law of my mind' and 'the law of sin which is in my members'

(7:23)—but now he speaks about a third principle, 'the law of the Spirit of life in Christ Jesus' (8:2a). Firstly, Paul affirms that in spite of the struggle, there is 'no condemnation' for the Christian—'no condemnation to those who are in Christ Jesus' (8:1a). We are justified by trusting in Jesus as our Saviour.

Some manuscripts omit the rest of verse one. If this is correct, the text should go straight on to speak about 'the law of the Spirit of life in Christ Jesus ... [which sets us] free from the law of sin and death' (8:2). In other words, we are justified by trusting in Jesus as our Saviour, but that's not all! There is a way of victory over the downward pull of the old sinful nature.

The 'law of the Spirit of life in Christ Jesus' is the principle of spiritual life flowing to us, springing up within us, by the power of the Holy Spirit, because we are in Christ Jesus our Saviour, and are united with Him in death and resurrection. The principle of sin is like the law of gravity pulling us down, but the principle of the Spirit of life in Christ Jesus our Saviour is like powerful rocket engines setting us free. This is very real. Often, we do feel pulled down, but we can cry to God for help and hope in Him. The Bible says that 'those who hope in the Lord will renew their strength. They will soar on wings like eagles; they will run and not grow weary, they will walk and not be faint' (Isaiah 40:31, NIV). This is the triumph of grace and that is the subject for our next study!

For further study ▶

'FOR FURTHER STUDY'

1. The New Testament speaks about the struggle Christians experience elsewhere. Look at Matthew 26:40–41; Galatians 5:16–18; 1 Peter 2:11; and 1 John 1:8–10.

TO THINK ABOUT AND DISCUSS

1. Has the struggle with sin, that you have experienced since becoming a Christian, ever made you wonder whether or not you were truly converted?

7 The triumph of grace

(8:1–39)

In this study, we learn about the power of the Holy Spirit at work in the Christian's life. We also learn about the glorious future and the ultimate triumph of grace, in accordance with God's plan and purpose, that cannot be thwarted.

The way of victory (8:1–4)

In the previous study, we saw that we are justified by trusting in Jesus as our Saviour, but that's not all! There is a way of victory over the downward pull of the old sinful nature. This is the meaning of the first two verses of chapter 8. The law of God, given through Moses, could not justify and give victory because of the weakness of sinful human nature, but God could and did by sending His Son (8:3–4):

- 'in the likeness of sinful flesh'—our Lord's human nature was real flesh, but not sinful flesh; He was the Lamb of God, 'without blemish and without spot' (1 Peter 1:18–19; also see John 1:14a)
- 'on account of sin'—i.e. to deal with sin by His death and resurrection

- 'He condemned sin in the flesh'—sin is a tyrant as we saw last time, but God condemned it to death at Calvary's Cross
- 'that the righteous requirement of the law might be fulfilled in us *who do not walk according to the flesh but according to the Spirit*'—the power of the Holy Spirit sets us free from the downward pull of the sinful nature ('the flesh' does not just mean our bodies but also the sinful nature that dwells in our bodies—see 7:17–20), though not without a struggle, as we saw in the previous study (see also Galatians 5:16–17).

The reason God sent His Son is so that 'the righteous requirement of the law might be fulfilled in us' (8:4a). Christians are not under the law (in the sense that the law no longer has any legitimate claim upon us because of Calvary's Cross), but when we walk in newness of life, we fulfil the law, by loving God and people (13:8–10; see also Matthew 22:36–40). This is another way by which the law is established (see 3:31).

However, it should be stressed that we only make a beginning in this life. Christians are often conscious of a struggle. The goal is not attained in this life. We should always be pressing on, not resting on our laurels but seeking to make progress by daily confessing and forsaking our sins (see Philippians 3:12–14; 1 John 1:8–9; Proverbs 28:13).

The new birth and the indwelling Holy Spirit are both needed (8:5–13)

The next few verses talk about what we *are*, not what we do. According to the Amplified Bible, verse 5 says that some people '*are* according to the flesh' and others '*are* according to the Spirit'. Verse 6 (NKJV) is the same—some are 'carnally minded' and some are 'spiritually minded'. It all depends on birth. Jesus said, 'That which is born of the flesh is flesh, and that which is born of the Spirit is spirit. Do not marvel that I said to you, "You must be born again"' (John 3:6–7). Until people are born again, they have no interest in 'the things of the Spirit' (8:5; see also 1 Corinthians 2:14). They are spiritually dead, hostile to God and His law and they cannot be anything else (8:6–7). Until people are born again, they cannot please God (8:8).

'*But*', says Paul to the Christians at Rome, God has intervened in your case—'you are not in the flesh but in the Spirit if indeed the Spirit of God dwells in you' (8:9). The 'if indeed' can be replaced by 'since' in the case of every genuine born-again believer—the Holy Spirit has been given to us (see also 5:5; Galatians 4:6). He makes His presence felt too. The principle of new life is at work in the Christian, overcoming the principle of sin and death—I believe this is the meaning of verse 10. Moreover, this way of victory in the *here and now* is only a foretaste of what will one day be ours when we have glorious resurrection bodies (8:11). Therefore, we owe a debt of gratitude to God to live for Him (8:12). The non-Christian way of life ends in death (8:13a), but Christians 'by the Spirit ... put to death the deeds of the body' in the here and now, and one day, when Jesus comes again, we will enjoy fullness of life and victory in glorious resurrection bodies (8:13b; see also 8:23).

The Holy Spirit gives us a joyful assurance of salvation (8:14–17)

The sons (and daughters) of God are led by the Spirit of God (8:14; see also 2 Corinthians 6:18). It is the Holy Spirit who leads, not the law. The law is 'the spirit of bondage again to fear', whereas the Holy Spirit is 'the Spirit of adoption by whom we cry out, "Abba, Father"' (8:15). In Bible times, being born into a family and being adopted were not mutually exclusive. The latter was to do with the inheritance. It was a legal ceremony acknowledging the person concerned to be the heir. No longer do we need to be scared of God's law. Instead, we cry out to our Heavenly Father (8:15) and the Holy Spirit gives us an inward assurance that the inheritance will be ours (8:16–17a). However, the bitter comes before the sweet. Do not be deceived! The Bible says we must expect suffering and trouble in this life, but glory beyond (8:17b; see also Acts 14:22).

The Holy Spirit gives us a joyful assurance of salvation. He is 'the Spirit of truth' (John 14:17a) and, *by means of the Word of truth*, the Holy Spirit enables us to understand the grace of God (Ephesians 2:8–9), to lay hold of the promise of God (John 5:24) and to know the joy of it (15:13). This is how it should be, but if we backslide into sin, the joy is lost (though not the salvation) until confession restores it (see Psalm 51:12; 1 John 1:4, 9).

The glorious future (8:18–25)

Returning to chapter 8, we have now come to a great climax. Christians are 'heirs—heirs of God and joint heirs with Christ' (8:17a). We are going to inherit the Glory (8:17b). It is true that the bitter must come first, but the glorious future far outweighs the painful present (8:18).

When Adam sinned in the Garden of Eden, the ground was cursed for his sake, death entered the world and the whole creation over which he had dominion was affected. Paul says that it was 'subjected to futility' (8:20a). However, the Bible also says that it was subjected 'in hope' (8:20b). The present ills of creation are not death throes, but 'birth pangs' (8:22). When Christians enter into the fullness of their salvation at the Second Coming, the whole creation will share in the benefits (8:19–21). Decay and death will be no more; the carnivorous nature of animals will be changed so that they can dwell safely together; the whole universe will be renewed; and 'there shall be no more curse' (Revelation 22:3). What a wonderful world it will be! The creation itself looks forward to this and so do we (8:23). When the Lord Jesus comes again, our bodies of sin and death will be changed into glorious bodies that will never sin and never die (see 1 Corinthians 15:51–53). This is when our sonship (or daughterhood) will receive full public acknowledgement, though even now the Holy Spirit assures us that it will be so because we have put our trust in the Lord Jesus Christ as our Saviour.

When we became Christians, we were saved *by* faith, but 'we were saved *in* this hope' (8:24a)—i.e. the glorious prospect that the apostle has been speaking about. Hope looks ahead to the unseen future and faith gives substance to our hope, making it 'sure and steadfast' (Hebrews 6:19a). This is why we are able to 'rejoice in hope of the glory of God' (5:1–2) and 'eagerly wait for it with perseverance' (8:25).

> Hope looks ahead to the unseen future and faith gives substance to our hope.

The Holy Spirit helps us to pray (8:26–27)

In the meantime, we experience 'weaknesses' and 'groanings' (8:26). This is because of the struggle with sin and 'the sufferings of this present time' (8:18), but the Holy Spirit helps in our weaknesses. He helps us to pray (8:26). This is very important because it is through prayer that we obtain the help we need. The groans are ours and the prayers are ours, but not apart from the Holy

Spirit—they are wrought in us by Him. Such prayers, even though ill-expressed, are sure to be answered because our Heavenly Father knows what is meant and these prayers are always 'according to the will of God' (8:27).

God's plan and purpose (8:28–30)

Christians struggle and suffer, but there is a good purpose in all the bad things that happen to us. 'All things', (even the bad things), 'work together for good' because God is working His purpose out (8:28). God's plan and purpose is that there should be a company of people, sometimes referred to in the Bible as 'the elect' (e.g. Matthew 24:22, 24, 31), composed of whoever is willing to trust in His Son, the Lord Jesus Christ. They have the firstfruits of everlasting spiritual life even now, and they will be raised up at the end of time to enjoy the fullness of the wonderful things that God has in store for them (see John 6:35–40). There are five steps by which God's plan and purpose is brought to fulfilment:

- Foreknowledge and predestination (8:29): God's plan and purpose was decided upon in eternity past. Before the dawn of time, before mankind even existed, God knew all about each one who would one day belong to Him and He planned our salvation (see also Ephesians 1:3–4a). This wonderful plan not only includes salvation from hell, nor even going to heaven when we die, but our destiny is 'to be conformed to the image of His Son, that He might be the firstborn among many brethren'! This happens progressively while we are here on earth and it will be brought to completion at the Second Coming. This is a big undertaking and it is no wonder that Christians have to pass through many difficult experiences. Finally, 'when He [the Lord Jesus Christ] is revealed, we shall be like Him, for we shall see Him as He is' (1 John 3:2)—a very pale reflection, no doubt, but something of Christ will shine out from every Christian.

- Called, justified and glorified (8:30): God calls us individually and powerfully by means of the gospel (see 1:16), and when we respond by putting our trust in the Lord Jesus Christ, He justifies us 'freely by His grace through the redemption that is in Christ Jesus' (3:24). The final step is future, but it is a certainty for those who are trusting in Him—'whom He justified, *these* He also glorified'. Paul speaks as though we have already arrived in the Glory, just as God, when promising to give the land of Canaan to Abraham's descendants, said, 'To your descendants I *have given* this land' (Genesis 15:18a), in spite of the fact that they would have to wait four hundred years before taking possession of it. It was that certain!

The doctrine of election is an awe-inspiring doctrine,

but it can also be a chilling doctrine, if mishandled. God has a mighty heart of love which 'desires all men to be saved and to come to the knowledge of the truth' (1 Timothy 2:3–4). He is 'not willing that any should perish but that all should come to repentance' (2 Peter 3:9). God loves *the whole wide world*; the sacrifice of Calvary is sufficient *for the whole wide world*; and the Lord Jesus Christ commanded that the gospel should be proclaimed *to the whole wide world* (see John 3:16; John 1:29; Mark 16:15).

Some Christians emphasise the doctrine of election and play down the truth of God's love for the whole wide world, while others emphasise the truth of God's love for the whole wide world and play down the doctrine of election. However, both are in the Bible and we should believe both. They may seem like parallel lines which never meet, but the Lord Jesus Christ brought these truths together very simply when he said, 'All that the Father gives Me will come to Me, and the one who comes to Me I will by no means cast out' (John 6:37).

Becoming a Christian is like coming to a door over which are the words, 'The one who comes to Me I will by no means cast out.' On the strength of this promise we go through the door, rejoicing that there is such a warm welcome for sinners. Then we look back and on the other side of the door we see the words, 'All that the Father gives Me will come to Me', and we are amazed to discover that we were one of that foreknown, elect company who were given to the Lord Jesus Christ before the dawn of time. As Dr Harry Ironside says, in his *Lectures on the Epistle to the Romans* [still available today as *Romans and Galatians*], these things are 'not for theologians to wrangle over but for saints to rejoice in'.[1]

Five unanswerable questions (8:31–39)

The whole doctrinal part of Romans is now brought to a triumphant conclusion by five unanswerable questions:

1. 'If God is for us, who can be against us?' (8:31b): The fact that God is for us is proven by 'these things' (8:31a)—i.e. the things that Paul has just been speaking about. The world, the flesh, and the devil are against us, but they are no match for God!

2. 'How shall He not with Him also freely give us all things?' (8:32b): The argument here is that God has already given 'His own Son' (8:32a). He is of infinite worth. The greatest gift has already been given, so, if we have received the Lord Jesus Christ, there can be no doubt that God will give us whatever else we need (8:32b).

3. 'Who shall bring a charge against God's elect?' (8:33a): This question looks ahead to the Day of Judgment. Charges could be brought, but what good will it do? God has already justified us (8:33b) and He is not going to change His mind (see Numbers 23:19a).

4. 'Who is he who condemns?' (8:34a): God the Father 'has committed all judgment to the Son' (John 5:22), but the Lord Jesus Christ will never condemn those who are trusting in Him. He is the very One who died to save us and even now He is interceding for us at God's right hand (8:34b).

5. 'Who shall separate us from the love of Christ? (8:35a): Shall the difficult times that all Christians go through? Or, how about the fierce persecution that some Christians have to face (see 8:35b–36)? 'No!' says Paul, 'in all these things we are more than conquerors *through Him who loved us*' (8:37, RSV). The love of God holds onto us through it all and enables us to triumph at last. The apostle assures us that there is nothing, nothing, *nothing* that is able 'to separate us from the love of God which is in Christ Jesus our Lord' (8:38–39). This 'love is as strong as death' (Song of Solomon 8:6). It is the strongest thing in the world. This is why Christians are eternally secure. As Jesus said, 'No one is able to snatch them out of My Father's hand' (see John 10:27–30).

From Him who loves me now so well

What power my soul can sever?

Shall life or death, or earth or hell?

No! I am His for ever.

(James Grindlay Small, 1817–88)

For further study ▶

'FOR FURTHER STUDY'

1. Weakness is never a problem, once we learn to depend upon our Saviour. His strength is made perfect in weakness. Look at 2 Corinthians 1:8–11; 3:4–6; and 12:9–10. Also, Philippians 4:13.

2. Some Christians emphasize the doctrine of election and play down the truth of God's love for the whole wide world, while others do the opposite. However, both are in the Bible, and we should humbly believe both. Look at Psalm 131.

TO THINK ABOUT AND DISCUSS

1. Have you ever made the big mistake of thinking you can live the Christian life in your own strength?

2. Are the parallel truths of election and the love of God for the whole wide world something you wrangle over or rejoice in?

8 The danger of perfectionism

Zealous Christians, in their eager desire for holiness, sometimes go too far. They imagine that it is possible to reach a state of sinless perfection in this life. This chapter provides a case study which shows the danger of this view.

I said in the last study that, 'Christians are often conscious of a struggle. The goal is not attained in this life. We should always be pressing on, not resting on our laurels but seeking to make progress by daily confessing and forsaking our sins.' Perfectionism is the opposite to this. It is saying that it is possible to reach a state of sinless perfection in this life. During church history, various individuals and groups have affirmed this. However, speaking personally, I believe that perfectionism is dangerous. I think many examples could be given to illustrate this, but I have decided to give just one—the experience of Harry Ironside during the early years of his Christian discipleship—he eventually became the pastor of the Moody Memorial Church.

Harry Ironside was brought up in a fine Christian home, associated with the Brethren Movement, and trusted in the Lord Jesus Christ as his Saviour as a boy of thirteen. He says that 'being saved myself, the first great desire that sprang up in my heart was an intense longing to lead others to the One who had made my peace with God.' In those days, the Salvation Army was at its spiritual zenith, devoted to going out after the lost. Harry's ardour matched theirs and he began his witness with them with such boldness that before long he was given the rank of junior sergeant major.

As well as going out after the lost, which was good, one of the distinctives of the Salvation Army was their teaching about holiness. Every Sunday morning, they held their 'holiness meetings'. Men and women spoke about receiving a 'second blessing' from God the Holy Spirit. They claimed that all indwelling sin had been 'burned out' of them and that they were as pure as unfallen Adam.

The testimonies seemed genuine and Harry, in the ardour of his love for the Lord, began to seek this experience. He gave up friends, pursuits, pleasures—everything he could think of that might hinder the incoming of the Holy Spirit and the consequent blessing. At last, one Saturday night, he determined to go out into the country and wait on God, not returning until he had received the blessing. He prayed in an agony for hours. Finally, he ended by crying, 'Lord, I give up all—everything, every person, every enjoyment that would hinder my living alone for Thee. Now give me, I pray Thee, the blessing!' He fell almost fainting to the ground. Then a holy ecstasy seemed to thrill all his being. He cried out in confidence, 'Lord, I believe Thou dost come in. Thou dost cleanse and purify me from all sin. I claim it now. Thy work is done. I am sanctified by Thy blood. Thou dost make me holy. I believe; I believe!' He felt unspeakably happy and hastened back to town so as to be able to testify to his experience at the 7 a.m. prayer meeting.

For some weeks after this, Harry lived in a dreamily happy state, rejoicing in his fancied sinlessness. In the past, when he had spoken at open-air meetings, he 'had always held up Christ and pointed the lost to Him', but now his own experience became his theme.

Gradually, he began to 'come back to earth'. As time went on, he 'began to be again conscious of inward desires toward evil—of thoughts that were unholy'. Going to a leading holiness teacher for help, Harry was told that it was not a sin to be tempted, so long as you do not yield to it. However, surely it was proof that all indwelling sin had *not* been burned out of him!

Harry was young and was kept busy going out to the lost. However, this unresolved tension simmered beneath the surface for the next five years. By this time, he was a captain in the Army, but he himself says that 'five years' active work ... had left me almost a nervous wreck, worn out in body and most acutely distressed in mind.'

At his own request, Harry was sent to the Beulah Home of Rest, near Oakland, California. There he found about fourteen Salvation Army officers broken in health, seeking recuperation. He says:

> Some were very godly and devoted. Their conscientiousness I could not doubt. But those who talked the loudest were plainly the least spiritual. They seldom read their Bibles, they rarely conversed together of Christ. An air of carelessness pervaded the whole place. Three sisters, most devoted women, were apparently more godly than any others; but two of them admitted to me that they were not sure about being perfectly holy. The other one was non-committal ... At last, I found myself becoming cold and cynical. Doubts as to everything assailed me like a legion of demons and I became almost afraid to let my mind dwell on these things.

Finally, 'a lassie-lieutenant, a woman some ten years my senior in age, was brought to the home ... I was much in her company, observed her closely, and finally came to the conclusion that she was the only wholly sanctified person in that place.' What a surprise was in store when this lady came to Harry, saying, 'I hear you are always occupied with the things of the Lord and I need your help!'

Harry thrust aside the secular book he had been reading and wondered what to do. He says, 'In God's providence a pamphlet caught my attention which my mother had given me some years before. In it the lost condition of all men by nature was emphasized. Redemption in Christ through His death was explained. Then there was much as to the believer's two natures and his eternal security, which to me seemed both ridiculous and absurd!' However, Harry was startled when the lassie-lieutenant exclaimed, 'O Captain, do you think that can possibly be true? If I could only believe that, I could die in peace!'

They both admitted to one another and to a third party who was present that 'we were *not* sanctified'. They 'now began to search the Scriptures earnestly for light and help'. Harry 'threw all secular books to one side, determined to let nothing hinder the careful, prayerful study of the word of God. Little by little, the light began to dawn ...'[1]

As we saw at the end of study five and the start of study six, there is no such thing in Scripture as the eradication of the old nature in this life. Yes, there is a way of victory, but I do not apologise for stressing once more that we only make a beginning in this life. As I said before, 'Christians are often conscious of a struggle.

The goal is not attained in this life. We should always be pressing on, not resting on our laurels but seeking to make progress by daily confessing and forsaking our sins.'

The quotations about the experience of Dr Ironside in the Salvation Army all come from his own book entitled, *Holiness—the False and the True*, published by Loizeaux Brothers in 1980. Much of this information can also be found in *Ordained of the Lord*, a biography by Dr E. Schuyler English, also published by Loizeaux Brothers in 1976.

In later life, although Dr Ironside never attained sinless perfection, he did indeed exhibit much holiness, so much so that when Dr English told Dr Ironside's daughter-in-law that he 'thought it would be foolish to pretend ... that [he] was perfect, she replied, "I know you're right, but it's hard for me to realize he was anything but perfect!"'[2]

'FOR FURTHER STUDY'

1. The pursuit of holiness is a good thing. Look at Matthew 5:1–10 and Philippians 3:7–16.

TO THINK ABOUT AND DISCUSS

1. How can we pursue holiness without falling into the trap that young Harry Ironside fell into?

9 The nation of Israel

(9:1–11:36)

When the Jewish people, as a whole, rejected their Messiah, everything seemed to go 'pear-shaped'. God's dealings with the nation of Israel are the mystery of the ages, but we are given a thorough explanation in the three chapters of Romans that we are about to consider.

This part of the epistle can be further subdivided as follows:

- How the Jewish people stumbled (9:1–33)
- How the gospel is now being proclaimed throughout the world (10:1–21)
- God's ongoing purpose for the nation of Israel (11:1–36)

Paul has been explaining how the gospel saves the sinner, but he has brought that subject to a triumphant conclusion. Now, he starts to speak about how the gospel relates to Israel. The word *Israel* (or *Israelites*) occurs thirteen times in these three chapters. It is the new name, meaning 'Prince with God', given by God to Jacob, the younger son of Isaac. The name was used to refer to the people descended from him and it is this people, this nation, which is the focus of the next three chapters. This is the big picture that we need to bear in mind as we look at these difficult but wonderful chapters.

How the Jewish people stumbled (9:1–33)

In Old Testament times, God's dealings with mankind centred upon the nation of Israel, but in the present Christian era, God's dealings with mankind centre upon the church. Does this mean that God is not interested in Israel anymore? 'Has God cast away His people?' (11:1). This is the question towards which the apostle Paul is heading. This is the question that he asks at the start of chapter 11.

Paul was Jewish and he starts by saying that he has a great concern for his 'countrymen according to the flesh', who had enjoyed such great privileges in Old Testament times (9:1–5). However, he goes on to point out, 'They are not all Israel who are of Israel' (9:6)—not all who were born of Israel's blood belonged to Israel as recognized by God. This is illustrated by the history of Abraham, Isaac and Jacob in the following verses (9:7–13).

The statement 'Jacob I have loved, but Esau I have hated' (9:13), which is a quotation from Malachi 1:2–3, may worry you, but it is no more worrying than our Lord's teaching that a Christian should 'hate his father and mother, wife and children, brothers and sisters, yes, and his own life also' (Luke 14:26). Obviously, Christianity is about loving people not hating them and a comparison with Matthew 10:37 shows that the 'hatred' urged in Luke is comparative rather than absolute. Likewise, it is reasonable to interpret the quotation from Malachi as being comparative, as well.

Another thing to bear in mind, is that Paul is now talking primarily about God's dealings with nations here on earth, not the salvation and eternal destiny of individuals. The quotation, 'The older shall serve the younger' (9:12), comes from Genesis chapter 25. It is part of what the Lord said to Rebekah when she was expecting Esau and Jacob—'Two nations are in your womb, two peoples shall be separated from your body; one people shall be stronger than the other, and the older shall serve the younger' (Genesis 25:23). So then, God favoured Israel more than Edom (the people descended from Esau). Was this wrong? 'Certainly not!' says Paul (9:14). It was a matter of mercy not justice (9:15–16; see also Exodus 33:19). God treats no one more harshly than they deserve, but to some He shows singular mercy.

By contrast, Pharaoh, the wicked tyrant who tried to prevent Israel from leaving Egypt, is a classic example of one to whom God did not show singular mercy. In this case, God's purpose was to 'show [His] ... power' (9:17). Yes, the Bible says that God hardened Pharaoh's heart (9:18; see also Exodus 7:3), but this was Pharaoh's fault not God's. The same Sun, which softens some things, hardens others—according to the nature of the object.

Likewise, the gospel, which softens the hearts of born-again believers, hardens those who reject it. This does not deny the culpability of those who reject this wonderful message (the Bible also says that Pharaoh hardened his own heart—see Exodus 8:15), nor does it mean that God desires such an outcome—'"As I live", says the Lord God, "I have no pleasure in the death of the wicked, but that the wicked turn from his way and live"' (Ezekiel 33:11a). However, God is the Potter and we are the clay—He has the right to make of us whatever He chooses (9:19–21).

He is the mighty God, the Lord of history. His judgments are to be feared and His mercies are most tender. In some cases, foreknowing the hard-hearted response, He chooses 'to show His wrath and to make His power known' (9:22a; see also Acts 15:18). Even then He shows 'much longsuffering' (9:22b). In other cases, He chooses to 'make known the riches of His glory on the vessels of mercy' (9:23). These 'vessels of mercy' are 'even us whom He called, not of the Jews only, but also of the Gentiles' (9:24). The inclusion of the Gentiles in the people of God was implied by Hosea (Romans 9:25–26;

see Hosea 2:23 and 1:10). Also, the exclusion of many of the Jewish people was plainly taught by Isaiah—only 'the remnant will be saved' (Romans 9:27–29; see Isaiah 10:22–23 and 1:9).

This is not arbitrary. Many Gentiles have been included because they have been willing to be justified by faith and trust in a crucified and risen Saviour (9:30), whereas many Jewish people have been unwilling (9:31–32a). Paul says, 'They stumbled at that stumbling stone' (9:32b). Again, this was predicted by Isaiah (Romans 9:33). The laying of the stone and the promise to believers is found in Isaiah 28:16. The fact that many in Israel would stumble over this stone is found in Isaiah 8:14–15.

The 'stumbling stone' is the Lord Jesus Christ. The reason most Jewish people 'stumbled' is because He was not the sort of Messiah they were expecting. They expected a conquering King, not a crucified Saviour (see 1 Corinthians 1:23). Of course, some Jewish people put their trust in the Lord Jesus Christ and to them He was 'a precious cornerstone, a sure foundation' (Isaiah 28:16), but most did not. They stumbled.

How the gospel is now being proclaimed throughout the world (10:1–21)

Paul did not stop praying for the Jewish people (10:1). The problem was that they did not understand the way of salvation. They did not understand the gospel of Christ (10:2–3; see also 1:16–17). They wanted to be justified by the deeds of the law, whereas Christians simply trust in the Lord Jesus Christ (10:4). The law is a *do* message (10:5; see Leviticus 18:5), whereas the gospel is a message about who the Lord Jesus Christ is and what He has done for us.

These chapters about Israel are full of quotations from the Old Testament. The Old Testament was a preparation for the New Testament. We need to understand the Old Testament in order to rightly understand the New Testament. In the next three verses, Paul quotes from Deuteronomy chapter 30, where Moses speaks about Israel's duty to 'do all His [God's] commandments ... which are written in this Book of the Law' (Deuteronomy 30:8–10). Moses points out that there was nothing 'mysterious' or 'far off' about the law. On the contrary, it was 'very near you, in your mouth and in your heart, that you may do it' (see Deuteronomy 30:11–14).

What Paul does in Romans chapter 10 is take the words of Moses and apply them to the gospel of Christ. There was no need for anyone to 'ascend into heaven', to obtain a revelation for mankind, because the Lord Jesus Christ has already come 'down from above' with precisely the revelation we need (10:6). There was no need for anyone to 'descend into the abyss' of the unseen world, to obtain a comforting message from the dead, because the Lord Jesus Christ has already come 'up from the dead', bringing life and immortality to light (10:7).

The gospel of Christ is a message that is 'near you, in your mouth and in your heart' (10:8)—'if you confess with your mouth the Lord Jesus and believe in your heart that God has raised Him from the dead, you will be saved' (10:9). Of course, how the gospel saves the sinner has already been set forth in the first eight chapters. This is just an abbreviated summary, similar to 'Jesus Christ and Him crucified' (1 Corinthians 2:2). Essentially, the gospel is in two parts—our Lord's wonderful Person and the atonement He accomplished for us by His death and resurrection.

When Paul speaks about confessing with the mouth (10:9–10), I believe he means the public confession of our faith and trust in the Lord Jesus Christ as our Saviour. This is what we do when we are baptized. As I said in study five, 'Baptism is commanded as a public testimony to our faith and as a sign of grace, but it does not confer grace. We are justified before God the moment we truly trust in the Lord Jesus Christ as our Saviour [as the first four chapters of Romans abundantly testify].'

This wonderful gospel is now being proclaimed throughout the whole world. The Jewish priority has ended; God has turned to the Gentiles and the great 'whosoever will, may come' message is going to the uttermost part of the earth (10:11–13; see also 1:16). The two great 'whoever' promises come from the Septuagint version of Isaiah 28:16 and from Joel 2:32. *Calling* on the name of the Lord is simply giving a voice to faith. As for *the name of the Lord*, it is 'Jesus' which means 'Saviour' (see Matthew 1:21). So, calling on the name of the Lord means expressing our faith in Him as our Saviour.

Of course, it is vital that God sends out preachers so that people can hear and respond to this wonderful gospel. Our Lord Jesus Christ compared gospel ministry to gathering in the harvest. Because 'the harvest is plentiful, but the laborers are few', He said that we should 'pray the Lord of the harvest to send out laborers into His harvest' (Matthew 9:37–38). Back in Romans, such labourers, such preachers, are said to have 'beautiful … feet' because the message they bring to people is such a good message (10:14–15; see also Isaiah 52:7).

The remainder of the chapter is taken up with the fact that people *have* heard the gospel, but not all have responded, especially the Jewish people (10:16–21). This was foreseen by the Old Testament prophets and Paul quotes from Isaiah 53:1, Psalm 19:4, Deuteronomy 32:21 and Isaiah 65:1–2. The pagan Gentiles were 'foolish'; they did not know much about the living and true God (10:19). Worse still, they were idolaters who did not seek Him. However, when they heard the gospel, many responded (10:20; see Acts 13:44; 48–49) and down through the centuries, this has continued to be the case.

Even though in Europe many are turning back to foolishness and darkness, there are still many millions turning to the Lord Jesus Christ, for example in Africa, India and China. By contrast, the Jewish people have proved to be, in the main, 'a disobedient and contrary people' (10:21). Throughout the gospel centuries, Jewish evangelism has been hard work.

God's ongoing purpose for the nation of Israel (11:1–36)

Does this mean that God is not interested in Israel anymore? 'Has God cast away His people?' (11:1a). This is the big question that chapters 9–11 ask and answer. 'Certainly not!', says Paul emphatically (11:1). He himself was a Jew who had responded to the gospel and he was not the only one. He refers to Elijah, who, in a time of depression, thought he was the only true believer left in Israel (11:2–3; see 1 Kings 19:10, 14), but was assured that there were 'seven thousand [others] who have not bowed the knee to Baal' (11:4; see 1 Kings 19:18). Even now, says Paul, in the present Gospel Age, 'there is a remnant according to the election of grace'

(11:5–6), and one day, as we shall see, '*all* Israel will be saved' (11:26).

The present situation is that the majority of Jewish people have stumbled and been blinded (11:7–10; see Isaiah 29:10; Deuteronomy 29:4; Psalm 69:22–23), but this is not intended to be permanent. 'Certainly not!', says Paul (11:11a). Yes, 'salvation has come to the Gentiles', but this is 'to provoke them [the Jewish people] to jealousy', that is, to cause them to want this wonderful salvation as well (11:11b).

In the next four verses, Paul anticipates a time when the Jewish people as a whole will know 'fullness' and 'acceptance' (11:12–15). The present situation is described as 'their fall', 'their failure' and 'their being cast away', and this has led to wonderful consequences— 'riches for the world', 'riches for the Gentiles' and 'the reconciling of the world'. In other words, because the Jewish people rejected their Messiah, the gospel of a crucified and risen Saviour is going throughout the world, bringing untold blessing (It was essential to God's plan of salvation that Jesus *should be* rejected and crucified at His first coming—see Acts 2:23). 'Now', says Paul, 'how much more' will the blessing be, if many Jewish people believe in Jesus.

This does not mean that the Old Testament Jewish primacy within the people of God will be reinstated. Paul explains what he means by comparing Israel to an olive tree. Some of the branches have been broken off because of unbelief, so that the Gentiles can be grafted in, but the Jewish people can be grafted in again, if they put their trust in Jesus (11:16–24). Robert Haldane helpfully speaks about the possibility, probability and certainty of their future conversion.[1] The possibility is mentioned in 11:23–'they also, if they do not continue in unbelief, will be grafted in, for God is able to graft them in again'. The probability is mentioned in 11:24–the argument here is that the grafting in of 'natural branches' is easier than the grafting in of branches from the wild Gentile olive tree.

As to the certainty, we will come to that in a moment, but first we should notice the warning to the largely Gentile church in 11:17–22. The apostle says 'do not boast ... you stand by faith. Do not be haughty, but fear ... He may not spare you either.' This does not contradict the eternal security of the genuine believer in the Lord Jesus Christ, which we saw in chapter 8. Rather, I think this is a warning to whatever professes to be the church of the Lord Jesus Christ here on earth. In the chapter entitled 'Justification by faith at the Reformation and later', I spoke about the destructive effect of liberal theology that was and is undermining the Christian faith in many theological colleges. Elsewhere, the danger is that people are being taught to put their trust in good works or outward things such as baptism, rather than having a personal faith and trust in the Lord Jesus Christ as their own Saviour. Another danger is when people 'turn the grace of our God into lewdness' (Jude 4) and say that, because we are saved by grace, it does not matter how we live our lives.

The certainty of the future conversion of the Jewish people is stated in 11:25. Paul says, 'Blindness in part has happened to Israel' (11:25), but this is only 'until the fullness of the Gentiles has come in' (11:25). God's wonderful purpose for the present age is that a great multitude should be saved from all nations (see Revelation 7:9–10) and should be included in His people, but, once they have 'come in', the blindness will be taken away 'and so *all* Israel will be saved' (11:26a), and not just a small remnant, as at present. I think this means that shortly before the Lord Jesus Christ comes again, there will be a great turning to Him among the Jewish people who are alive and remain at that time. Many will put their trust in Him and be saved—this is the 'fullness' spoken of in 11:12. This is supported by the quotation from Isaiah 59:20—when Jesus comes again, He 'will turn away ungodliness from Jacob' (11:26b).

There are many other passages in the Old Testament that could be quoted in support of this idea of the future conversion of the Jewish people (e.g. Jeremiah 23:5–6; Zechariah 12:10). However, it is only right to point out that some theologians do not accept this idea. Dr Martin

Luther's *Commentary on Romans* was translated into English by Dr J. Theodore Mueller and he comments that:

> Luther at first wavered with regard to the conversion of 'all Israel'. In Romans he at times speaks as though he believed in the final conversion of all Jews, though he also emphasizes the fact that only the elect will be saved. Later he definitely accepted the opinion of Origen, Theophylact, Jerome, and others, who identified 'all Israel' with the number of the elect, to which corresponds the expression 'the fulness of the Gentiles'. The leading Lutheran exegetes have followed this interpretation and taught that while the elect from among the Gentiles are being brought in through the preaching of the Gospel before Judgment Day, so also are the elect from among the Jews.[2]

That is all right as far as it goes, but there has always been a small remnant of genuine Jewish believers, whether in Elijah's day or Paul's day. It seems to me that to say we can expect nothing more than this goes against the whole flow of the argument in chapter 11. God chose the Jewish people in Old Testament times and this is 'irrevocable' (11:28–29). The fact that they stumbled means that the disobedient Gentiles 'have now obtained mercy through their [the Jewish people's] disobedience' (11:30)—the glad message of a crucified and risen Saviour is now going to all the nations of mankind, including the disobedient Jewish people, many of whom will also share in this mercy (11:31). 'For God has committed them all to disobedience that He might have mercy on all' (11:32). This sounds strange, but it means that God has permitted and caused things to happen in such a way that all, whether Jew or Gentile, have no alternative but His mercy and grace, which is abundantly available to all through the gospel. That all should receive it is the desire of His mighty heart of love (see 1 Timothy 2:3–4).

This causes Paul to marvel at the wisdom of God's ways with mankind (11:33). 'God moves in a mysterious way His wonders to perform', as the hymnwriter, William Cowper (1731–1800), says. The three unanswerable questions in 11:34–35 come from Isaiah 40:13 and Job 41:11. No one would ever have guessed what God was going to do. No mere human being could ever have invented the gospel. God is indebted to no one. On the contrary, He is the one who offers His free mercy to all. He is the beginning, the middle and the end of everything *and to Him belongs the glory forever* (11:36). Amen!

Great God of Abraham! hear our prayer;

Let Abraham's seed Thy mercy share:

O may they now at length return

And look on Him they pierced, and mourn!

Remember Jacob's flock of old;
Bring home Thy wanderers to Thy fold;
Remember too Thy promised word,
'Israel at last shall seek the Lord.'

Though outcasts still, estranged from Thee,
Cut off from their own olive-tree,
Why should they longer such remain?
For Thou canst graft them in again.

Lord, put Thy law within their hearts,
And write it in their inward parts;
The veil of darkness rend in two,
Which hides Messiah from their view.

O haste the day, foretold so long,
When Jew and Greek, a glorious throng,
One house shall seek, one prayer shall pour,
And one Redeemer shall adore!
(Thomas Cotterill, 1779–1823)

'FOR FURTHER STUDY'

1. There are many passages in the Old Testament which could be quoted in support of the future conversion of the Jewish people. Look at Isaiah 59:20; Jeremiah 23:5–6; and Zechariah 12:10.

TO THINK ABOUT AND DISCUSS

1. Should the conversion of the Jewish people have a special place in our prayers as Christians?

10 The Christian life

(12:1–13:14)

In this study, we move from theory to practice. Christianity is not only believing the great truths of the gospel, but also living a life in keeping with what we believe.

Having explained the mystery of the ages—God's dealings with Israel—the apostle Paul now moves on to speak about the practical outworking of the new life that we have in the Lord Jesus Christ. This final part of the epistle can be further subdivided as follows:

- The Christian life (12:1–13:14)
- Doubtful things (14:1–15:7)
- Closing remarks (15:8–16:27)

An appeal to consecration (12:1)

The practical part of Romans begins with an appeal to consecration, based on what Paul calls 'the mercies of God' (12:1). Paul has been speaking about these 'mercies', which are abundantly available to both Jew and Gentile through the gospel, in chapter 11. However, it is chapters 1–8 which set forth in detail what these mercies are—the wonderful plan of salvation by grace through faith in the Lord Jesus Christ; the wonderful atonement which He accomplished by His death and resurrection.

The appeal here at the start of chapter 12, is to those who are already Christians ('brethren') and it is an entreaty rather than a command, because God wants us to give our lives to serving Him gladly and not because we think we have to (see 2 Corinthians 9:7). However, it is very 'reasonable' (12:1) because, as the great cricketer and pioneer missionary C.T. Studd put it, 'If Jesus Christ be God and died for me, then no sacrifice can be too great for me to make for Him.'[1]

Consider the mercies of God. We are sinners, lost and undone (3:9), yet God has set forth a way by which we can be declared righteous before Him, simply by trusting in the Lord Jesus Christ as our Saviour (3:28). If we do this, then sin's power over us is broken (6:14) and glory awaits us (8:18)! God is for us (8:31–33); the Lord Jesus Christ makes intercession for us (8:34); and nothing can separate us from the love of God in Him (8:35–39). Above all, consider the great price that was paid to make all this possible—'Christ died for us' (5:6–8). The hymn writer, Samuel Crossman (1623–83), rightly says: 'O who am I, that for my sake My Lord should take frail flesh, and die?'

In view of all this, how can we hesitate to give our lives wholly to God? How can we hold anything back? The sacrifice that is called for is 'a living sacrifice' (12:1) or *a sacrifice while we are still alive.* Certainly, we should be willing to die for our God and Saviour, but here we are called to live for Him. Our bodies have so often been the vehicle of sin, but now they should be 'holy, acceptable to God', and they can be. Like all that is commanded or entreated in the New Testament, this appeal to consecration is an implied promise to the Christian. By God's grace, it can be done (albeit imperfectly).

Being transformed by the renewing of our mind (12:2a)

The next verse speaks about being 'transformed by the renewing of your mind' (12:2a). What we think about is very important. Philippians 4:8 urges us to 'meditate on' or *think about* things which are true, noble, just, pure, lovely etc. There is a strong connection between what we think and what we are. For example, Proverbs 23:7, speaking about an evil man, says, 'For as he thinks in his heart, so is he', and this verse before us in Romans, speaking about Christians, says that we should 'be transformed by the renewing of … [our] mind'. Do you want to be true, noble, just, pure, lovely etc? Then think about such things!

This is not easy. This is a battle for the mind. Christians

are sometimes greatly distressed by evil thoughts, even when they are praying, and they sometimes wonder whether they are really converted or not. Christians love the Lord Jesus Christ and we want to follow Him, but indwelling sin often makes its presence felt in this way. It is very distressing. However, it should not make true believers doubt their salvation. The fact that we are distressed is evidence that we are saved.

John Bunyan also knew what it was to be troubled by evil thoughts and he sought to depict this in *The Pilgrim's Progress*. He tells us that Christian had to go through a grim valley called the *Valley of the Shadow of Death* and it was night-time. Moreover, 'one of the Wicked Ones got behind him, and stept up softly to him, and whisperingly suggested many grievous Blasphemies to him, which he verily thought had proceeded from his own mind'. This greatly distressed Christian. However, he was encouraged to believe that God was still with him (see Psalm 23:4) and 'by and by the Day broke: Then said Christian, He hath turned the Shadow of Death into the Morning,' and he had sunshine the rest of the way through the valley.[2]

Returning to the verse before us in Romans, it also says that we should not be 'conformed to this world' (12:2a). The Bible does not condemn contact with the world but conformity to it. We are to be *in* the world, but we are not *of* the world (see John 17:11, 15–16). We are sent into the world with God's Word and this is what protects us (see John 17:17–18). It is not just having or even reading the Bible that protects us, but God working through it to change our thinking and thus transform us.

What God wants us to do (12:2b–8)

The apostle speaks about proving 'what is that good and acceptable and perfect will of God' (12:2b). Nothing can be better for us than to be in the centre of His will, and if we have a consecrated life and a renewed mind, we will be able to discern what God wants us to do.

There are general good works which all Christians should do, but there are also special good works which vary from Christian to Christian. Paul starts, in the next verse, by saying that we should think about what God wants us to do for Him, guarding against having too high an opinion of ourselves (12:3). Then he goes on to say that God's people are 'one body in Christ', but that in a body each member has a different role (12:4–5). For example, the mouth does the speaking, the hands do most of the work and the feet take the body to places. Each Christian has a part to play and work to do, and each Christian is given sufficient grace to do what God wants him or her to do (12:6a). Seven examples of special good works are given in 12:6b–8, but this list is not exhaustive.

Once we have discerned the special work that God

wants us to do, we should give our strength to it and do it the best we can. We may not have to look far. As Solomon wisely says, 'Whatever your hand finds to do, do it with your might' (Ecclesiastes 9:10).

All that we do should be marked by love (12:9–16)

God wants us to work and also to 'love' (12:9a). The latter is very important (see 1 Corinthians 13:1–3; Revelation 2:4; John 21:15–17). Love must be genuine (12:9a), holy (12:9b) and humble (12:10). When we show such love to one another (12:10), we are 'serving the Lord' (12:11; see also Matthew 25:40) and such service should be marked by zealous activity and a fervent spirit (12:11).

The pressures of life tend to cool the fervency of our love (see Matthew 24:12), but our sure hope for the future should keep us joyful, persevering and prayerful (12:12). Geoffrey Wilson rightly comments that 'prayer is the means ordained of God for the supply of grace sufficient'[3]—see also Luke 18:1.

Finally, Paul says that love must be practically expressed—e.g. by generosity or hospitality (12:13; see also 1 John 3:18). This should be shown especially to 'the saints', but also to all people (see Galatians 6:10). We should seek to be a blessing even to those who persecute us (12:14) and, in general, we should seek to meet people where they are—whether they are rejoicing, weeping or just humbly plodding on in life's way (12:15–16).

We should not seek to avenge ourselves (12:17–21)

Christians are entitled to seek justice from 'the governing authorities' (13:1; see also Luke 18:2–3), but we must not take matters into our own hands (12:17a). To maintain this high standard is part of our Christian witness (12:17b). We should make every effort to 'live peaceably with all men' (12:18) and refrain from avenging ourselves (12:19a). Vengeance belongs to God (12:19b).

Therefore, Christians should show grace and do positive good to their enemies (12:20a; see also Matthew 5:44). If they are unmoved by this, their judgment will be increased (12:20b), but it may turn them into friends (12:21). This is what happened in our case, when God reconciled us to Himself through the death of His Son (see 5:10–11).

Our duty as citizens (13:1–7)

Christians have dual citizenship. Even though Christians know that 'our citizenship is in heaven' (Philippians 3:20), we also have a duty to whichever earthly country we belong. Submission to 'the governing authorities' is commanded (13:1). God rules in the affairs of men and He has raised up the governing authorities for some good purpose, even if they are 'the basest of men' (Daniel 4:17 KJV; see also 9:17). This is why Paul says we should submit to them (13:2).

Resisting the governing authorities leads to temporal (not eternal) judgment (13:2b). Rulers have teeth and fear of punishment is one reason for submission. However, in the main, obeying the government should not trouble our consciences—even bad rulers do not usually punish good behaviour (13:3). On the contrary, a ruler is 'God's minister' (13:4) and we *should* obey them (13:5), *except when they tell us to disobey God* (Acts 5:27–29).

We should obey the government and also pay for it (13:6)—God has ordained it to punish the evildoer, so that 'we may lead a quiet and peaceable life in all godliness and reverence' (see 1 Timothy 2:1–2). We should pay our taxes and show due respect to everyone (13:7; see also Matthew 22:15–22).

Paul wrote this epistle from Corinth. Greetings from some of the Corinthian Christians are included at the end. One of these was 'Erastus, the treasurer of the city' (see 16:21–23). Clearly, becoming a Christian had not led to him abandoning his public duties. A Christian on the town council or the local school's board of governors can be a good thing, so long as we are faithful to what is right and do not compromise with evil.

Our duty to love our neighbour (13:8–10)

Beyond our duty as citizens, we have a duty to 'love one another' (13:8a). Christians are 'not under law' (6:14), but they fulfil the law because they are motivated by love (13:8b). By contrast, those who rely on doing good works to obtain salvation do not fulfil the law because they act 'grudgingly or of necessity', which is not what pleases God (2 Corinthians 9:7).

Paul quotes those of the Ten Commandments that define our duty to other people and says they 'are all summed up in this saying, namely, "You shall love your neighbour as yourself"' (8:9; see also Leviticus 19:18 and Matthew 22:34–40). If I genuinely love my neighbour, I will not wish to do him or her harm (13:10a).

Likewise, if I love God, I will want to give Him the place in my life that is rightfully His. I will not want to bow down to idols, take His name in vain or disregard the Lord's Day. This is why 'love is the fulfilment of the law' (13:10b).

The Second Coming is getter nearer every day (13:11–14)

Paul goes on to say that 'the night is far spent' and 'the day is at hand' (13:11–12a). By 'the night' he means the present Gospel Age. 'The day' refers to the Second Coming and the fact that it is 'at hand' means that it is time to be up and doing (13:11a). God has already decided when the Second Coming will be (see Acts 17:30–31) and it is getting 'nearer' every day (13:11b).

We should live in the light of this day of days by

casting off all that belongs to the darkness and putting on the Christian armour (13:12b). This includes casting off intemperance, impurity and bitterness (13:13), and also '[putting] on the Lord Jesus Christ', whose salvation protects us like armour in the spiritual warfare (13:14a; see also Ephesian 6:10–20). Let us trust in Him wholeheartedly as our Saviour and make good use of 'the sword of the Spirit' (Ephesians 6:17) and the weapon of 'all prayer' (Ephesians 6:18).

Finally, Paul says, 'Make no provision for the flesh, to fulfil its lusts' (13:14b). Because of our union with the Lord Jesus Christ in death and resurrection, sin no longer has any legitimate claim on us and we should give our lives wholly to God, as we saw in study five (see 6:11–14). We should do nothing which gives 'the flesh', the old sinful nature, an opportunity to express itself.

For further study ▶

'FOR FURTHER STUDY'

1. Seven examples of special good works are given in Romans 12:6–8, but this list is not exhaustive. Look at 1 Peter 4:7–11 to see what Peter says about this subject.

2. A Christian serving the community can be a good thing, so long as we are faithful to what is right and do not compromise with evil. An example of the former is Daniel, the faithful, whereas an example of the latter is Lot, the compromiser. Look at Daniel 1:1–21 and Genesis 13:5–13.

TO THINK ABOUT AND DISCUSS

1. Do you lack vitality in your Christian life because you have no special work to do for the Lord, no outlet of blessing to others?

2. Are you ever tempted to compromise with evil?

11 Doubtful things and closing remarks

(14:1–16:27)

There are many things about which the Bible is crystal clear, but there are also some things for which this is not the case. In this study, the apostle gives us principles by which we can handle such issues well. In his closing remarks, he also shows how much he appreciates his fellow believers.

Doubtful things (14:1–15:7)

In Romans chapter 14, the apostle Paul begins to speak about people who are 'weak in the faith' (14:1). This does not mean someone who is too weak to believe the fundamental truths of the gospel, nor someone too weak to resist temptation, but someone too weak to grasp the full implications of Christian liberty. Such people should be welcome in our churches (14:1) and should not be despised (14:2–3a).

When God gave his law to Israel at Mount Sinai, it included commandments concerning what they could and could not eat. Perhaps this explains why the main example given is food (14:2). In the present Christian era, God has declared all foods 'clean', but it is understandable that some Jewish Christians, because of their background, may have doubts (Acts 10:13–15). Paul says that the one who doubts should not eat (14:23). This is the way to maintain a clear conscience.

When Christians are perplexed about what to do, they should avoid doing things about which they have doubts, but they should not judge other Christians who do those things (14:3–4). The other Christians may be 'fully convinced in ... [their] own mind' that what they are doing is permissible (14:5). This is the way to avoid becoming fault-finding and ungracious.

The next example Paul gives is observing special days (14:5–6a). Contrary to modern calendars, Sunday or *the Lord's Day* is the first day of the week. It was on this day that the early Christians 'came together to break bread' (Acts 20:7), and it was on this day that they set aside money to meet the needs of God's people (1 Corinthians 16:1–2). It perpetuated the principle of a weekly work–rest cycle which was commanded by the law (see Exodus 20:8–11).

When speaking about special days which some Christians observe and others do not, the apostle probably had in mind certain additional days on which, according to the law, 'no customary work' was to be done (Leviticus 23:5–8, 23–25). However, we could also apply this to Christmas and Easter, and some Christians are stricter about observing the Lord's Day than others. The point is that even when we disagree about such matters as food and drink and observing special days, true believers are united in wanting to please the Lord Jesus in all that we do (14:6–9). It is not our place to judge other Christians about such matters, nor to despise them (14:10–12), but rather to avoid whatever may hinder them (14:13).

Actually, the Bible teaches clearly that all foods are 'clean', as we have already seen (see also 14:14a; Mark 7:18–19; Colossian 2:16–17). However, 'whatever is not from faith is sin' (14:23), and we should avoid using our liberty in an irresponsible way by urging weaker brothers and sisters to go against their consciences (14:14b–16; see also Galatians 5:13).

The blessings of 'the kingdom of God' are spiritual and we should major on such things (14:17–19; see also Ephesians 1:3). Unimportant matters such as food and drink should not be allowed to harm the work of God (14:20–21). Also, there is a danger of allowing things that really are sinful, so even the strong need to be careful (14:22), and certainly the weak should not be urged to go against their consciences, for 'whatever is not from faith is sin' (14:23).

Finally, Paul sets before us the example of the Lord Jesus Christ who was willing to endure even the reproaches of the ungodly (15:1–3). Think of all the hostility and mockery that He quietly endured as He trod the path to the Cross. He 'did not please Himself' (15:3a) and neither should the strong, who are only being called upon to 'bear with the scruples of the weak' (15:1–2).

Paul's quotation from the Old Testament (15:3; see Psalm 69:9) leads to the general remark that the Scriptures were written for our benefit, encouraging us to persevere and giving us hope (15:4). Such patience and encouragement come from God and Paul prays that God will enable us to show this patience and encouragement 'toward one another', leading to unity and praise to God (15:5–6).

Therefore, whoever genuinely trusts in the Lord Jesus Christ as their Saviour and gladly acknowledges Him as their Lord should be welcome in our churches, regardless of his or her convictions on lesser matters (15:7).

Closing remarks (15:8–16:27)
What I have referred to as 'Closing remarks' can be further subdivided as follows:
- Paul's ministry to the Gentiles (15:8–33)
- Many greetings (16:1–24)
- Closing doxology (16:25–27)

Paul's ministry to the Gentiles (15:8–33)
Salvation was promised 'to the fathers' (i.e. the fathers

of the Jewish people) and this was confirmed by the ministry of the Lord Jesus Christ (15:8). However, God's mercy has reached out to the Gentiles and they too are included, as was foretold by the prophets (15:9–12; also see Psalm 18:49; Deuteronomy 32:43; Isaiah 11:10).

The final quotation speaks about the Gentiles hoping in Christ (15:12) and Paul turns this into a prayer, saying, 'Now may the God of hope fill you with all joy and peace in believing, that you may abound in hope by the power of the Holy Spirit' (15:13). This is a prayer that Christians should enjoy their salvation to the full (see John 10:10). The only condition of salvation is 'believing' (trusting) in the Lord Jesus Christ, but a believer can fall short of the abundant life and the full enjoyment of salvation. Let us pray that we will not (see Luke 11:13; 1 John 1:4).

Although Paul has prayed for them to be 'filled', he now expresses his confidence that the Christians at Rome '*are* full of goodness, filled with all knowledge ...' (15:14). However, he has written this great epistle to them 'because of the grace given to me by God' (15:15). This was not saving grace but serving grace (15:16a). Paul was 'called to be an apostle' (1:1), along with the eleven apostles chosen by the Lord Jesus Christ during His earthly ministry (excluding the traitor, Judas Iscariot). However, out of all the apostles, it was Paul who was chosen supremely to be the apostle 'to the

Gentiles' (15:16a; see also Acts 26:17–18; Galatians 2:7–9).

Paul refers to himself as 'a *minister* of Jesus Christ to the Gentiles', but he goes on to qualify this. He was not *ministering the sacraments*, but 'ministering the gospel of God'. His ministry did not involve *the offering of sacrifices*, but 'the offering of the Gentiles ... sanctified by the Holy Spirit' (15:16b).

Paul glories in 'what Christ has accomplished through me' (15:17–18, NIV). This included 'mighty signs and wonders', but the main thing was 'the power of the Spirit of God' wonderfully changing lives (15:19; see also 1:16; 1 Corinthians 6:9–11), often in previously unevangelised areas (15:20–21; see also Isaiah 52:15). This is why he had been 'much hindered from coming to [Rome]' (15:22), but now he planned to 'journey to Spain', and this meant he could visit Rome en route (15:23–24).

However, first he was 'going to Jerusalem' (15:25) to take a gift from Gentile believers 'for the poor among the saints who are in Jerusalem' (15:26)—this was indeed appropriate (15:27). Then he hoped to 'go by way of you to Spain' and he was sure that the 'gospel of Christ' would be a blessing to those in Rome (15:28–29), but he asked for prayer, because he was aware of the hostility of the unbelieving Jewish people to his ministry (15:30–32).

Finally, he prays once more for them, saying, 'Now the God of peace be with you all. Amen' (15:33).

Paul *did* eventually arrive in Rome, albeit as a prisoner, about three years later. The interesting story of how prayer was answered is to be found in Acts chapters 20–28. It is believed that Paul was subsequently released and perhaps he did indeed visit Spain, before being imprisoned again and executed in Rome in AD 67, according to Ussher.[1]

Many greetings (16:1–24)

The apostle Paul was not an austere theologian, remote from the lives and feelings of ordinary people. In this final chapter, he shows how much he appreciated his fellow believers.

The chapter begins by mentioning 'Phoebe our sister' (16:1). As I said in the chapter entitled 'Background and summary', 'The epistle is thought to have been written when Paul was in Corinth ... It may well be that a woman named Phoebe was the bearer. She was "a servant of the church in Cenchrea", which is near Corinth, and she had business of some sort to transact in Rome' (16:1–2). The greetings begin in verse 3. Clearly, the apostle knew quite a number of the Christians at Rome and everything he says about them is warm and positive (16:3–15).

He encourages them to express their affection for one another (16:16), and we should do the same, though I think we have the freedom to use a kiss or handshake or whatever is appropriate in our culture. Only, whatever we do, let it be 'holy' and set apart from anything unhelpful.

I think it is a lesson to us that everything Paul says about genuine Christians is warm and positive. No Christian is perfect. It is always possible to find fault, and yet he does not. However, the apostle realises that not everyone who attends a local church, not everyone who professes to be a Christian, really is. He knows about *wolves in sheep's clothing* (see Matthew 7:15). This is why he warns the Christians at Rome to 'note' and 'avoid' such people (16:17).

This great epistle contains a wonderful and comprehensive explanation of the message of salvation (the gospel)—this is 'the doctrine which you learned' (16:17). Those who hold to anything contrary to this are to be noted and avoided. The marks of such people are:

- they are divisive and cause some to stumble (16:17a)
- they promote false teaching (16:17b)
- they are concerned about gratifying their appetites (16:18a)
- they sound convincing to new believers (16:18b)

Paul had heard good reports of the Christians at Rome, but he wanted them to be discerning about such matters (16:19)—just as the Lord Jesus warned His disciples to 'beware of false prophets' (Matthew 7:15; see also Matthew 10:16).

Behind such teaching and people stands Satan. However, the decisive battle has already been fought and won (Colossians 2:13–15) and the war will soon be over (16:20a). In the meantime, by 'the grace of our Lord Jesus Christ', we can be victorious (16:20b).

Paul believed in team ministry. He often refers to his fellow workers in his epistles. Here, 'Timothy, my fellow worker' joins in sending greetings to the Christians at Rome (16:21a). Likewise, 'Lucius, Jason, and Sosipater, my countrymen, greet you' (16:21b).

Paul usually dictated his epistles, adding a few words in his own hand at the end to authenticate what was written (e.g. 2 Thessalonians 3:17–18). In those days, letter-writing was a distinct profession. In this case, the amanuensis was 'Tertius' who also sends greetings (16:22).

Finally, 'Gaius, my host and the host of the whole church [at Corinth], greets you. Erastus, the treasurer of the city, greets you, and Quartus, a brother' (16:23). Erastus was 'the treasurer of the city', whereas Quartus was only 'a brother', but the fact that you are 'a brother [or sister]' is all that matters in the church (see Matthew 23:8).

When Paul added a few words in his own hand at the end of his epistles, to authenticate what was written, he invariably referred to 'grace'—the free, unmerited favour of God. This was the essence of the message he proclaimed. He had already done this in verse 20 and now he refers to 'grace' again in verse 24 (some manuscripts omit verse 24, but the majority include it). Perhaps this was when he took the pen from Tertius.

Humanly speaking, Paul may have intended to end the epistle at this point, but the greatness of the gospel and the wonder of the mystery of the ages fills his heart and he is moved by the Holy Spirit to add a closing doxology, which is a worthy ending to this magnificent epistle.

Closing Doxology (16:25–27)

This is addressed to 'Him who is able to establish you'. The gospel is about God's ability, not ours. He is 'able to establish … [us] according to':

- 'my gospel and the preaching of Jesus Christ'—this is what Romans is about: the message of salvation by the wonderful grace of God through faith in the Lord Jesus Christ
- 'the revelation of the mystery kept secret since the world began but now made manifest, and by the prophetic Scriptures made known to all nations'—this is the mystery of the ages by which God permitted the Jewish people to reject their Messiah so that the glad message of a crucified and risen Saviour could go to all nations and save

millions, including the many Jewish people who would one day believe in Jesus

- 'the commandment of the everlasting God, for obedience to the faith'—we are obedient to the faith the moment we believe the gospel and put our trust in the Lord Jesus Christ as our own Saviour

This is how God establishes us: He justifies us by faith and trust in the Lord Jesus Christ; He brings us into friendship with Himself; and He causes us to stand, supported by all the resources of His grace:

To God, alone wise, be glory through Jesus Christ forever. Amen. (16:27)

For further study ▶

'FOR FURTHER STUDY'

1. The Bible says that some things are clearly revealed whereas others are not. Look at Deuteronomy 29:29.

TO THINK ABOUT AND DISCUSS

1. Do things which are not crystal clear in the Bible cause problems at your church?

Endnotes

Introduction

1 Luther, Martin [Translated by J. Theodore Mueller], *Commentary on Romans*, (Grand Rapids, Michigan: Kregel Publications, 1976), p. xiii (Luther's preface)
2 Tyndale, William, *William Tyndale's New Testament* (Ware: Wordsworth Editions Limited, 2002), p. 249
3 De Haan, Richard W., *The World on Trial: Studies in Romans* — Classics, (Grand Rapids, Michigan: Zondervan Publishing House, 1970), p. 9

Background and summary

1 Foxe, John, *Foxe's Book of Martyrs* (Grand Rapids, Michigan: Kregel Publications, 2016), p. 33
2 Ussher, James, *The Annals of the World*, (Arkansas: Master Books, 2008), p. 863
3 Baxter, Dr J. Sidlow, *Explore the Book*, (London: Marshall, Morgan & Scott, 1966) Part VI, p. 69

Chapter 1: The Gospel

1 Wilson, Geoffrey B., *Romans, A Digest of Reformed Comment*, (Edinburgh: Banner of Truth, 1984), p. 19
2 Haldane, Robert, *Commentary on Romans*, (Grand Rapids, Michigan: Kregel Publications, 1996), p. 57

Chapter 4: Justification by faith at the Reformation and later

1 Bainton, Professor Roland, *Here I Stand: A Life of Martin Luther*, (Peabody, Massachusetts: Hendrickson Publishers, 2012), p. 48
2 Haldane, Robert, *Commentary on Romans*, p. 7
3 Ironside, Dr Harry, *Lectures on the Epistle to the Romans*, (New Jersey: Loizeaux Brothers, 25th Edition, 1982); available today as *Romans and Galatians* (Grand Rapids, Michigan: Kregel Publications, 2006)
4 Ironside, Dr Harry, *Lectures on the Book of Acts*, (New Jersey: Loizeaux Brothers, 1982), pp. 430–431

Chapter 5: Consequences and an explanation

1 Wilson, Geoffrey B., *Romans*, A Digest of Reformed Comment, p. 81
2 McIntosh, Professor Andy, *Genesis 1–11*, (Leominster: Day One Publications, 2016)

Chapter 6: The struggle

1 Wilson, Geoffrey B., *Romans, A Digest of Reformed Comment*, p. 120

Chapter 7: The triumph of grace

1 Ironside, Dr Harry, *Lectures on the Epistle to the Romans*, p. 106

Chapter 8: The danger of perfectionism

1 Ironside, Dr Harry, *Holiness— the False and the True*, (New Jersey: Loizeaux Brothers, 1980), pp. 13,17,19–20,25,29–31
2 English, Dr E. Schuyler, *Ordained of the Lord*, (New Jersey: Loizeaux Brothers, 1976) pp. 203–204

Chapter 9: The nation of Israel

1 Haldane, Robert, *Commentary on Romans*, p. 548
2 Luther, Martin, *Commentary on Romans*, p. 162

Chapter 10: The Christian life

1 Alford, Timothy, 'C. T. Studd (1860–1931)', *Evangelical Times*, Nov 2010, p. 27
2 Bunyan, John, *The Pilgrim's Progress*, (Edinburgh: Banner of Truth, 1990), pp. 68–69

3 Wilson, Geoffrey B., *Romans, A Digest of Reformed Comment*, p. 204

Chapter 11: Doubtful things and closing remarks

1 Ussher, James, *The Annals of the World*, p. 875